Praise for "Love, Sex, Nakedness and the Divine"

My nickname for Keith is the 'Love Man'. In his book of, what I would describe as a series of 'Love Essays', Keith is brave enough to write about taboo topics, like Sex and Nakedness and he does it from a place of total unconditional Love and understanding. My favourite line of his is, 'We came from Love, we are Love and we're in the process of returning to Love'.

This book will have you examine your own relationship with Love, the Love you have for yourself, most importantly. This is not just a book, it's a manual, a blueprint and a search engine that will have you wishing and wondering how you also can step into that Divine Love and Wisdom that Keith shares with us all. Enjoy!

Michael de Groot - @stayingaliveuk. www.StayingAliveuk.com

One of the sweetest books about Love to date. Keith Higgs looks at love from every possible angle and keeps showing us over and over again how and why to do it. All you need is love!

Laurie Handlers - MA...author, film producer, sex and happiness coach. www.ButterflyWorkshops.com

In 'Love, Sex, Nakedness and the Divine' Keith Higgs has bravely and skilfully created a book about, what is in my opinion, the greatest need of our world today, i.e., how to return to Truth, Oneness and Love. "There is only Love" he (continually and eloquently) points out, and "that Love is us."

Through four powerful lenses (Love, Sex, Nakedness and the Divine) Keith paints a picture of our current world as a crazy illusionary dream, made up of fear, regret, separation and false truths. He clears a path from these back to the reality of true Love.

I invite everyone to travel this amazing path back with Keith. It is lined with truly captivating, Spirit-infused language, which has been birthed from Keith's own inner searching, experiences of life and authentic dances with Spirit.

Both an invitation and a challenge to embrace the cosmic story of Love leap off every page of this beautiful book.

Rose O'Mahony

Keith once again proves himself to be the master of that sacred ground where spiritual psychology meets Tantra. You might say it's the Kama Sutra meets A Course In Miracles.

Michael Day – KingofTarot

Keith's latest book is filled with beautiful quotes and inspiring messages and reminders on how to open to Love more in our life.

He gently invites us to look at ourselves honestly and see where we can let go and invite even more Love and connection. Beautiful, inspiring, tender, and deeply insightful. Read it with an open heart and even more open mind and discover just how much Love is waiting for you.

Sy and Ash - BeMore@syandash.co.uk **www.syandash.co.uk**

Keith has devoted much of his life in the search and exploration of this abstract term called Love—the Love of self and sacred union of the soul and the cosmos. He has distilled down collective consciousness into a pocket plan for mortal beings to follow and then brought them with a bang of Love rocket fuel to this new age, and onto and through these pages. He has made gateways and access points, stripping away the construct and constraints of shame by bravely addressing the taboo subject of nakedness with the knife blade of his penned truth. Words that can cut away any false illusions we have lived under.

Along with his own unique expression which he has channelled and scribed wonderingly, to give a mix of poetry meeting quantum physics. Harvesting the science and transforming into introspective rhymes for this time.

If you want, hitch a lift, ride and bravely go where mankind has not managed yet to climb, on the wave lengths of the high vibration of Love. This is the best guide in the galaxy. It gives short cuts in a concise cosmic journey map and will help you avoid the worm holes that others have taken.

I invite you to engage with this book and ride the wave lengths of Love.

Ann-Marie Avery - Msc (Applied Behavioural Science)

An absolutely wonderful book to help us understand our body and our sexuality.

Devaraj Sandberg - Osho Leela Personal Development Centre **www.OshoLeela.uk**

*Ed?. Best wishes on your journey back to Love
Big Love + Thanks
Keith*

Love, Sex, Nakedness and the Divine

By Keith Higgs

Messages from Love to Empower and Enlighten Your Journey

#LSND #FlyBacktoLove #TheLittleBookofLove #KeithHiggs #Love

Copyright © 2018 by Keith Higgs

ISBN:
  Paperback: 978-1-9997319-2-2
  eBook: 978-1-9997319-3-9

All rights reserved. No part of this book may be reproduced or transmitted in any form or by any means, electronic or mechanical, including photocopying, recording, or by any information storage and retrieval systems, without permission in writing from the copyright owner.
Rev. date 25/07/18

To order additional copies of this book contact:
Awake Your Dreams Books
+44 1799 610600
www.LSND.info
orders@AwakeYourDreamsBooks.com
or purchase through www.LSND.info

CONTENTS

Acknowledgements i
Introduction ii

PART ONE: LOVE 1
   Love – The All Encompassing Energy of the Divine 2
   All You Need Is Love 4
   Self Esteem 6
   Self Love 9
   The Mirror 10
   Affirmations 11
   Do You Love Yourself? 12
   Giving is Love and Love is Giving! 14
   Removing the Blocks to Love 16
   Am I My Body? 18
   Reach Out 19
   A Letter to a Lover 21
   Where Have All The Kisses Gone? 24
   Love Shines through the Tears 26
   A Birthday Message from Love 27
   A Message from Love 29
   Self Love – Sacrifice or Selfishness 30
   The Golden Rule Love! 32

PART TWO: SEX 35
   SEX 36
   Sex, Nudity, Freedom, and the Divine 39
   Tantra or Tantric Sex 41
   Tantra 41
   Tantric Sex 43

A Quick Spurt of Pleasure 44
Boundaries or Blocks? 46
An Ode to the Goddess 47

PART THREE: NAKEDNESS 49
Nakedness 50
Waking Up Naked 52
Skinny Dipping 54
An Apology to Our Genitals 56
Come to Me 58

PART FOUR: THE DIVINE 61
Valiant Explorers 62
No Longer a Caterpillar 65
Revealing Jewels 67
Love is the Breath of the Divine 69
A Part of the Divine 71
Words from the Divine 74
The Divine 75
How Can I Serve? 77

Some Questions and Reflections 79
In Conclusion 80
Connections 81
Recommended Reading 82
About the Author 83
Other Books by Keith Higgs 84
Online Course 86
Notes 87

taste of a state of being, which is worth striving to keep; the way, by passing through all the healings and forgiveness needed to stay in or return to that place of bliss?

Sex: The moment of full orgasm is the closest thing to stepping into bliss, forgetting the body in a heavenly place of ecstasy. Sex can be a gateway to a different state. Sex is loved, hated, feared or desired, and so many people seek to control it. Yet often it's almost uncontrollable. It creates incredible power and life it itself. Sexual energy is one of the most powerful forces in our beings.

Nakedness: Being truly naked is the essence of being, dropping everything that hides and all the walls that surround our hearts. It is becoming totally open. It is about dropping shame and fears. It is not just about physical nakedness, though that can also be liberating, and a picture of freedom.

The Divine: Another label or name for the Supreme Being. It is a name, possibly without as many dividing prejudices as those associated with, God, Allah or Jehovah or the many other names given by different religions and belief systems. It is my choice; please substitute whatever name feels best for you. In my belief system, this is just a name or label for the magical power of Love, which is the One and All things. You can choose; it is all about the experience, feelings and beliefs. These are so much more than any human words can hold.

This book contains, I hope for you, ideas thoughts and practices to help you experience Love, Sex, Nakedness and the Divine, in a different light and profoundly deeper ways.

satya - truthfulness

the divine, universe, God = LOVE

he could certainly know what would take place; and hence, in the order of cause and effect, he must decree in order to know." It is readily conceded, that, in the order of nature, the Divine Being could not foreknow that a world would certainly exist, until he had determined to create it. But was there no prescience back of this? Did he determine to create a universe, independent of a view of all the bearings in the case? If so, he created at random and in ignorance. If not, then a view of all the results preceded his determination to create; and thus we are led irresistibly to the doctrine of the sermon, that "God foreknows in order to predestinate,"

[3] The review of the sermon, in the Christian Spectator, is understood to be from the pen of Doctor Fitch, professor of divinity in Yale College.

[4] See Christian Spectator, Vol. iv, No. 3.

[5] A part of this sermon has lately been published, in a tract form, and circulated with the *avowed* purpose of counteracting the influence of the sermon "on predestination."

[6] A man was afflicted with the hydrophobia. When his paroxysms were coming on he was aware of it, and gave warning to his friends to be on their guard, that he might not injure them. Suppose, however, he knew of a sure remedy, but voluntarily neglected to avail himself of it. Would he not in that case be guilty, not only of all the evils that might result to others from his malady; but also of self murder? And yet this man's madness was entirely beyond the direct control of his will.

ACKNOWLEDGEMENTS

This book is dedicated to You.

To all the parts of us—of me. To those of you, I have loved, to all that I have forgotten to Love. To those of you I have held close, to all I have, so far, not held close. To those I have met and all I am yet to meet. To those, I remember and all those I have so far forgotten.

I bathe each part of us in Love and forgiveness, all I have created and all I have denied. I love you all and look for the absence of time, where we will again all be living in the knowledge of our oneness. Let's take our stories and these messages and wrap them all together, and then follow their paths into heaven, here and forever.

Big Love Keith.

P.S. Special thanks to Michael de Groot, Rose O'Mahony and everyone who inspired, advised, commented, and helped with the birth of this book.

INTRODUCTION

Untold beauty, through words of Magic Love, has touched and often surprised me, some at times of deep sorrow and grief, and others, at times of joy or questioning.

Always the Light of Love comes shining through with its answers. It brings messages of hope, peace, and Love, often in the early hours of the morning.

Where do these messages come from? That's a question I have often asked—from the Divine, from the collective mind, from deep inside, from the wellsprings of Love.

These words have touched, frequently melted my heart and brought me back to places of Love, gratitude, and joy. It is my pleasure to share them with you in the hope that some of them will resonate and bring you similar joys, answers, Love and many other blessings.

They are given in Love and sent with Loving energy.

Your servant, in Love Keith.

Love, Sex, Nakedness and the Divine

It's a strange and sad thing that these words have had their meanings corrupted, denigrated and many taboos attached. Warning bells ring, yet desire is also aroused within to find out more.

Let's look at each one in their purity and see how they can set us free, bring pleasure and even enlightenment.

Love: Love they say is a momentary madness soon to depart or a state of emotions boosted by bodily chemicals running wild, but what if it was actually moments of heavenly connection, a remembering of our true state and a stepping into a place of paradise, with another; an experience designed to give us a

PART ONE

LOVE

*'We are beings of Love and
the only reason we are here is to Love.'
– Marianne Williamson*

*'Only when you have found peace within yourself
can you help us find peace for the entire world.
Every person is a brother or sister of a great
family of many thousands of years.
When one person does an act of kindness,
all our hands extend with his or hers.
If one person should fall, all of us stumble.
If one suffers we all feel pain.
When one rejoices, we are all uplifted.
In our oneness we will find our destiny
and our destiny is to be one.
For we are a single body breathing
with a single set of lungs,
pulsating with a single heart,
drawing from a single well of consciousness.'
We are One. Let it be with Love.
– Tzvi Freeman*

PART ONE: LOVE

Love – The All Encompassing Energy of the Divine

*'Divine Love play me as an instrument in
Your finely tuned orchestra of Life.' – Kristine Carlson*

Love surrounds us in its many forms. From the morning warmth of a new day's sunshine to the warm glow of an evening fire which is overlooked by a cosmic band of sparkling starlight sharing its incredible celestial beauty. The sound of playful children laughing. The passion of lovers with energy darting between their eyes, moving to passionate embrace and the ecstasies of lovemaking, lost in moments of pure bliss. The beauty of a flower, which is opening, waiting, hoping to be pollinated and bring forth fruit, to be part of the creation of more of its own. The unselfish love of a mother for her child. She is often sacrificing her time, health and even life, to give life, protect and nurture her offspring.

There are many beautiful pictures in our world of this all-encompassing and Divine Energy. We can look in amazement at its power. It is a force that can't be measured and is only seen through its effects, and through its manifestations, through objects and beings in this physical realm.

Our Sun is a perfect picture it continually expends its all-powerful energy, sending warmth and light into the universe and to our planet. It seeming receives nothing in return, constantly giving. We on, our planet, are placed in a perfect location, not too close and not too far away to receive the ideal temperature range necessary for our well being and survival. Could all this be coincidence or are these all wonderful pictures and signs for us, so we can see and recognise the beauty and wisdom of this Divine Love?

There are many facets or types and pictures of Love, but they all seem to have similar messages of beauty, connection and giving.

We are told the Golden Rule, or only law is to Love, and without Love we are nothing. So what could we be, but Love incarnate looking to experience and enjoy itself and its all-encompassing power?

If we truly open our eyes and shed any false imposed beliefs and fears, what lessons and messages can we see, in these very pictures, and in nature and life? What conclusions can we come to?

My conclusion: We are the offspring of that incredible force of Love, the Power that is Everything. Sometimes we make mistakes and become mischievous children, but we are still loved, nurtured and protected as a part of the vast family of humanity. We are headed towards an eventual reunion and understanding of our true natures. What is your conclusion?

In Spirit, when we shed our mortal pictures, ideas, illusions, and human skins, along with the cloaking of our bodies in this life and dimension. We too are the Energy of Love.

Again, at the deepest level, this is All there is!

PART ONE: LOVE

All You Need Is Love

'The Greatest of these is Love.' – The Bible

The Beatles sang it, or just repeated it. So many wise men, prophets, scholars, authors, poets, scientists, and just ordinary people, have echoed it. This simple, yet profound message, comes, broadcasting in, throughout time, from the annals of history and reaches us today.

I believe it to be the most quintessential truth one can discover. Why else would we journey through this planet and solar system? Nature cries it! We circle a hot sun; a ball of almost unlimited energy, without it life would cease to exist. Its very essence and energy is the magical component of the growth of every plant and again, the building block of all life. Our earth's position is ideal. We orbit perfectly in a place between a cold frozen wasteland and a fiery hell. This too is a picture of Love. If we stray too far, to either side, we can burn up in the fires of jealousy or have our heart wither in a cold, lonely, frozen desert.

We can't see love, or can we? We can feel its warmth in a smile and see its effects and the changes created by its energy. It can warm a life and melt the hardest heart. Yet often we isolate ourselves against it for fear of being hurt or being consumed by all the changes it can bring.

Healing modalities use its power. They are sending the power and vibration of love from one heart and being to another. Sending it, through time and space, to touch another beings stuck energy and resonate together, so both can once more vibrate in unison with the very nature of things, which is Love.

Religious texts teach us that if what we do is without love, we are nothing. I believe God, Spirit, Energy and any other label you would like to give the Divine, is Love. In fact, as scientists have proved that everything is energy, it is then easy to interpolate that all things are energy. We are part of those All Things. This is the magical place where science and most spiritual teachers meet. We are a part of God! Our root being and our core is Love. Maybe we have to journey there, through many dark ages of our own creation, seeking so many other ways to come back to this fundamental truth.

As we seek to live it, through personal growth or spirituality, I believe we can reconnect with the entirety of ourselves. Realising the Kingdom of Heaven, or Bliss, or Nirvana, is within. Again, substitute this with whatever label or word picture you prefer. All the projections or the hologram of our thoughts without are just a playground, a world experience, giving us choices and many learnings on our route back to discovering, realisation, and the owning of what we have been, and in essence, are all along.

I believe the only law in creation is to Love, as some would say; 'God's only Law is Love!'

How we play out these earthly roles now and in the illusions of pasts and futures are of no significant consequence to the greatest truth that we are, and I am, the loving energy that comprises all things!

PART ONE: LOVE

Self Esteem

'Self-respect, self-worth and self-love all start with self. Stop looking outside yourself for your value.' – Rob Liano

One of the most significant human issues facing so many of us in different degrees and flavours is low self-worth or low self-esteem. Too many children, in a moment of anger or even minor accident, have been told by frustrated, harried parents they are clumsy, useless, stupid or worse. These messages have often been repeated—so many times that they have, on a certain level been believed and therefore become a part of our reality.

These messages are often further compounded by teachers in school and their often careless remarks or scolding. That very belief system can become a badge of dishonour. This badge, unless actions are taken to remove it, can be worn for a lifetime. By nature, some who suffer from this mental abuse manage to rebel against this programming, and it can make them stronger. Sadly others succumb and often repeat these beliefs to themselves in their mental chatter and frequent thoughts. That belief system then, unless freed, holds them back throughout their lives.

What are you saying to yourself, especially at times of challenge or change, when faced with particular tasks or seemingly unpleasant situations? Frequent little thoughts may seem like friends who protect and keep us safe, but actually, they are creating colossal self-harm. They are stifling opportunities to succeed, in their own favourite areas of self-denial and uncertainty.

These thoughts and personal disempowering mantras, if not routed out and replaced with self-confidence and empowering beliefs will hold us back or even destroy our mental health leading to breakdown or despair.

Never fear all things are possible everything can be changed, and every fear rooted out. There are many tools, processes, aides and willing helpers to enable us to overcome anything. The first step is recognising the issue or beliefs that hold us back, most now entirely subconsciously. No belief or self-imposed truth is permanent, and we are, underneath all this previous powerful negative programming, actually incredibly powerful amazing Divine beings—though most of us have forgotten this for a while.

It is time to remember again, to dwell in restored empowering beliefs and walk in our magnificence and full power!

What does that take?

Self Love, Self Belief, Self Esteem. Sadly in the past, many people have had these powerful states drummed out of them, often told they were proud, too loud or too pushy. While there is a balance, these are vital characteristics for success in almost every endeavour, from relationships to business via every other human experience and especially in any form of decision making. Are you weak in any of these areas? Or in some cases do you overcompensate, with false bravado or an over pushy attitude, then collapsing into well-hidden fears when no one is around to notice?

First, realise it! You are okay and in fact very special. You have vast resources of endowed special gifts and talents. You are unique, and under it all, especially under those previously adopted badges of shame, you are a powerful, amazing, beautiful being! So now it is time to cut off and throw away all those old badges, the thoughts and belief systems that hold within them all your disempowerment.

Now a warning, don't say it is too hard or difficult. That is also a negative belief, held as a safety net by those same insidious beliefs, as a last stand against their soon to be departing disempowerment. Many people have dropped those old patterns in an instant of transformation. If you'd like, you can too!

So, how about it? Would you like to let the old thoughts and programming go? It isn't a part of the powerful being that is you, just some tatty old safety blanket, grabbed in desperation, many years ago, now totally unfit for the new and beautiful you, now emerging as a new creature, from an old stifling past.

Whatever your old beliefs entailed, many others have overcome similar beliefs you are not alone. So it is just a choice. Are you ready now?

Even if it is not plain exactly what the root issue is, your

PART ONE: LOVE

subconscious knows. The desire to grow, overcome and prosper again is enough for the miracle of transformation to work its magic.

The decision to LET GO is all it takes!
Are you ready now?
Yes?
Great!
It is done!
Let's celebrate, in gratitude and belief.
It is done!

Now it may take, and I would recommend reinforcing that change with some positive steps and actions and especially new beliefs but for now, just believe. The miracle of transformation has already happened in that instant that you truly desired it and let go.

The next sections contain three powerful tools for keeping building on the foundations of that change and strengthening all that you have chosen. The newly restored you that is now emerging from the rubble of all past defeats and insecurities. That new you needs to hold on to the security of the knowing, that the old has passed. It is time to assimilate and enforce new beliefs with feeding, empowering and strengthening doses of Self Love, appreciation and affirmation.

So let's move entirely into the place of the new or should we say restored being, the wonderful you, that under all those old imposed weights has always been magnificent anyway.

Never forget, ever again, that you are, in Spirit, and have always been an amazingly powerful Divine being. Now it is the time, in our destiny and evolution, for that being to come back to the surface and shine, revealing its power and true destiny. Let's Go!

Self Love

> *'You are a precious soul with a divine essence.*
> *A luminous spiritual being having a human experience,*
> *filled with lessons and opportunities for growth,*
> *acceptance and self-love.'* – Kris Carr

We have just broken through with the miracle of transformation, into the world of Love, Light, and Spirit. Just like the little bean seed that I have just been watching. In the early stages of its growth, that little bean has pushed through the darkness of the heavy soil, its birthing place, raising its head out of that darkness into a new realm of sunlight and the beginning of a priceless new day.

What is the first thing it does? It unfurls is tiny new budding leaves and then turning towards the light, opens them to receive the warmth of that sunlight. It starts using that energy and absorbing it. Mixing it along with nutrients attracted from the earth, it is rapidly growing in its new realm of being. It is getting ready to grow and bring forth much fruit and many more beans.

So likewise in our process of change, we must keep opening to the light and basking in the warmth of its Love, mixing that with the nutrients of lessons learnt on this earthly voyage. The energy of that Love, when mixed with our learnings, will propel and strengthen our being in the new realm of growth and light.

In the past, those chattering voices of self-abuse have held us back in their darkness. Now it is time to replace them with the different voices of Love, Gratitude, and Forgiveness and especially with the certainty of knowing we are both Loved, and also composed of the very essence and energy of that Love itself. We are Love!

One of the ways to cement and feed this new belief system, to grow it in this new state of being is Self Love. A quick word of warning. Make sure you don't let this become selfishness, as this is not what self-love is about. There is a delicate balance to be upheld, as true Love is also always about giving.

PART ONE: LOVE

The Mirror

[handwritten note: mirror work + affirmations for releasing doubt, fear + shame]

Have you ever stood in front of a mirror and looked into the eyes and heart of the amazing beautiful being there, and said with compassion and deep Love, "I Love you?"

If not—it is time to start, and if so, it could be time to do it more often. This practice is a fantastic tool for boosting confidence, building compassion and beginning or continuing the journey of growth for your tender new being.

It can be extremely challenging at first, like standing naked for the first time in front of a stranger. Old patterns of embarrassment and low self-esteem seem to want to run to the front and shout out their old refrains! Resist them and look deeper. Let the amazing power of the Love inside you triumph. It always can! Resist the urge to run, or close your eyes. Look deep, and with warm eyes of hope and belief and say: "I Love YOU!"

Repeat this time and time again, daily, or even more often, until this new Love affair has grown into an empowering bond and habitual belief. Deep Love, and self-respect, a knowing that will never again be shaken.

You, Yes, You are amazing! You are healing in your power and new beliefs. Even while still standing on the earth, you are flying speedily back to your home, in the Heavenly Realm of Love. You are becoming whole again—soon never to stray into the darkness of the fears, thoughts, and beliefs of other realms. For you are Love!

Your tender new being will need constant love, affirmation and nurturing to help it continue to grow in new beliefs, habits, and strengths. Keep feeding it with positive mind-changing information from heavenly thoughts and realms.

Repeat this beautiful practice of mirror work until it becomes a habit. Write yourself Love and appreciation letters. Make lists of your accomplishments, and successes, and you will soon come to believe the truth that you are and always have been amazing, even in spite of a few, now forgiven, mistakes along the way.

Affirmations

Old patterns of thought need to be overwritten with new empowering programmes and beliefs. One of the powerful ways to do this is with powerful, positive affirmations, meditation, and frequent thoughts of your new truths.

Suggestion: Make a list of all your old repeated mind chatters, their favourite sayings and demeaning diatribes. After the next step, cross them out or better yet burn them. Make another list, on another piece of paper, or the other half of the first sheet, of all the diametric opposites of those old disempowering statements and false beliefs. This part is for you to keep.

If it was, "I am weak," write down and frequently repeat, "I am strong!"

If it was, "I am sick," write down and frequently repeat, "I am healthy!"

If it was, "I am useless," write down and frequently repeat, "I am useful!"

If it was, "I am ugly," write down and frequently repeat, "I am beautiful!"

You get the point. Search out your egos old favourites and replace them all with positive thoughts and empowering affirmations.

So many old "I Am's!" These were patterns of negative vibrations, disempowering habits, holding you back in fears and darkness. Their replacement and its practice will now build new neural pathways, patterns of thought and new beliefs that will empower and speed your journey back into the light.

There are many more ideas and tools to help understand, create awareness, and help with this transformation, in my first book, "Take Control of Your Spacecraft and Fly Back to Love - a Manual and Guidebook for Life's Journey."

PART ONE: LOVE

Do You Love Yourself?

'Self-love is not selfish; you cannot truly love another until you know how to love yourself - Unknown

If you met yourself at a party or a networking event would you want to get to know you?

How about if you were the opposite sex, or if you prefer the same sex, would you want to have a date or even make love with you?

Do you feel good about you?

Can you look in the mirror and deep into the eyes and heart of the beautiful being there and feel deep Love and respect.

Can you stand naked in front of that mirror, and love the being there, and feel good? – And not be critical and especially not self-loathing?

Can you love yourself and every part of your being so much that you can bring yourself to ecstatic orgasms of body, mind, and spirit?

If the answer to any of these is no, or even I'm not sure, then it is time to do something about it! These are most certainly some of the blocks that are holding you back big time in many areas of life.

Are love, wealth, success and deeper relationships all held back or are they crumbling into eventual failure, due to flawed habits, hidden resentments and the falsehoods of guilt?

Know nothing is insurmountable, and the miracle required is only a change of thought or attitude and beliefs. Beliefs are just thoughts repeated over and over until they become strong cords of opinion and the habits of habitual thought, neural nets or pathways that our mind and ego have been drawn to walk repeatedly down.

Self-love can and frequently must begin with self-forgiveness and also, in most cases, the forgiveness of others. Any bitterness fermenting inside is only, like caustic soda, damaging the vessel that holds it.

It is time to stop and take stock of all that is going on within, The pathways of thought, the habits of thinking or the frequent thoughts we are accepting as ours, are they really what we want? Are they creating the beauty and Love that our hearts desire, or are they keeping us in the cold recesses of a damaged loveless world?

It is never too late to turn around and look to Love. You can find it inside. That is the miracle of a change of thought and direction.

Where are the vibrations of your energy taking you? Are you solidifying into stuck patterns of depression and defeat, slowly freezing you heart, clogging the flow of your life force and your spirit within. Or are they ever cleansing, faster flowing and deepening the joy, inspiration, and your Love?

A change of direction is just a decision, a letting go. Sometimes, when really stuck, change works best when mixed with the washing of sincere, heartfelt tears. This is an exercise in belief, Love and forgiveness. Then make the actions to compound that decision. It's time to choose to continue in that new direction and to overwrite old thoughts, old habits, and programmes.

This may take the form of a daily practice, the repetition of new thoughts or affirmations of success and self-worth. Come back to the mirror and see in the eyes and heart of your being, a new creature with tender sprouts of renewed Love growing inside. Nurture and water them with the kind thoughts of acceptance and gratitude. The power of belief and faith creates the change, enhancing the desire of your life force for growth and Love.

You are a divine being. Your core after all, old thoughts, lies, and habits are washed away, is pure Love. Tenderly love that beautiful inner being. It has been there all along, though sometimes starved by a lack of Love and recognition. The inner you is now growing and prospering again. You are being led along ever lightening paths, towards a date with your ultimate destiny, in a place with no more hurt or sorrow, just the pure joy of the ever-increasing blissful dance of perfect Love.

PART ONE: LOVE

Giving is Love and Love is Giving!

'Love grows by giving. The love we give away is the only love we keep. The only way to retain love is to give it away.' – Elbert Hubbard

We are Love and Loves highest manifestation is giving. Why are we still here in this realm, or more accurately, even though we are awakening and realising we are actually a part of another realm, why do we still perceive our place in this earthly realm?

There are still lessons for us, of realisation and of the errors that we sometimes hold onto. There are also many learnings about giving, being the Light, Love and a sample of forgiveness, of holding no grievances or malice. Our mission is showing pure Love to all those that we perceive as being still in this realm with us. It is healing old grievances; so that we can walk together again in Love and dissolve the chains that hold us back in this illusion and often seeming darkness.

It is about transforming the experience of this realm into the heaven it could and can be, where Love is sown in place of strife and grievances are healed. There is no place in the realm of Spirit for any disharmony. All of those grievances must be dissolved for all of us to enter the Kingdom of Love.

It is hand in hand that we enter that Kingdom. We will do it together with all the perceived separate parts of us, which are still waiting to become one with us again. Loves sacrifice is giving, forgiveness and thus salvation for all.

There is no room for selfishness or holding on to ideas of being right—that is just self-righteousness. Love gives unconditionally with the realisation that all it sees is a part of itself. It gives Love, acceptance and of itself until all is made right again. It gives whatever it takes—until all the monsters in the room dissolve and become loving, gentle creatures playfully walking in harmony and peace.

The Kingdom of Love is then restored. Heaven and Love rule in both realms and all illusions are dissolved into oneness again. Our part in this grand design is just to give Love, Be Love and Receive Love. Yes, giving Love comes first. Give Love and compassion to yourself and all the beings you meet along the

LOVE, SEX, NAKEDNESS AND THE DIVINE

way, whether beasts and fiends or friends and Lovers, understanding that all are one and just parts of the whole and especially mirrors of the unloved parts of us.

How would you treat your children, even at times of mischief or mistake, or your brother or sister? Even if much-polluted water has passed under the bridge, it is time for the forgiveness of our misperceptions and grievances. It is time for the healing of our relationships and reuniting of our hearts again in the One Love. Being all we truly are. This is the only route back to Love! All beings are crying for it!

When we can see that each act we perceive is either an act of Love or a cry for Love, we are getting very close to returning again to the place of our home where our highest Spirit always abides— in the Heart of Love.

Keep Loving, touching and bringing all unloved parts back together. We will meet again soon and find we are there together, in that wondrous place of Eternal Love.

the more you love unconditionally, the more will come back to you.

PART ONE: LOVE

Removing the Blocks to Love

'Happiness is more about removing the blocks to Love and remembering who you are than changing your situation or another person.' – Lee L. Jampolsky

I had a powerful experience in the early hours of the morning today. Another significant piece of the jigsaw puzzle of this incredible life jumped up, revealed itself and showed up as a key piece of understanding and growth. Just like when making a jigsaw puzzle we can get stuck or delayed for awhile searching for that vital piece—and the knowledge of how and where it fits with all the other pieces around it. The understanding of this piece, I had already known, but I had not realised the fullness of its significance, as a key pivotal truth.

Interesting after meeting and connecting briefly with Marianne Williamson the day before—one of her central teachings that I have always loved is. We don't need to find Love; we just need to remove all of our blocks to it. "Love is what we were born with. Fear is what we have learned here. The spiritual journey is the relinquishment—or unlearning—of fear and the acceptance of love back into our hearts."

I had been drawn to a book that I purchased at the Hay House I Can Do It event. "Finding Your Soul Mate with Theta Healing," by Vianna Stibal. I was inspired to see much of her message about the causes of our stuckness and issues in life held similar conclusions to my own. I shared much about that in my first book "Take Control of Your Spacecraft and Fly Back to Love - a Manual and Guidebook for Life's Journey." It is all about how our automatic programs, or autopilot, are what is holding us back. It has tools and ideas sharing how to reprogram these limiting beliefs and automatic reactions.

The magic and significance is that she considers these too as blocks and shares the way to overcome or as Marianne would say melt them, is to open up to the feeling of the opposite emotion of the particular block by connecting with the loving energy of the Divine or God. Thus letting that perfect energy wash and melt away each belief or block. These blocks were once established for our protection and when dissolved free us to align once again with the Divine Love that we are.

Now I don't know all the procedures suggested and I haven't, (when writing this,) finished the book and would feel that all the intricacies of that method are just one way to experience this powerful melting, cleansing and core belief reprogramming. However I can say just meditating or running the affirmations and beliefs through my consciousness led to some powerful cosmic orgasms of connected bliss, belief, confirmation and a renewed confidence that all things are indeed possible and moving rapidly into my world.

Starting to read this book was a wonderful experience; with I'm sure, more to follow as I explore this inspired book.

? chakra healing...?

PART ONE: LOVE

Am I My Body?

> *'I am not my body. My body is nothing without me.'*
> *– Tom Stoppard*

Love is above, around and beyond this limited dream world of illusion. Our super being, our essence, our spirit inhabits that place, rather than just the earthly dimension that our senses now perceive. We have become so focused and embroiled in this world that most of us don't remember our true home and aren't conscious of our real place of being.

Imagine if you worked at NASA and your mission was controlling the Mars rover. You work in a fantastic place full of all the latest technology, people, and incredible things. However, your focus is totally looking through a couple of cameras out onto an alien landscape, hearing the sounds of the planet and the machine through your headset, and through gyroscopes and sensors feeling every bump and incline in your individual control pod. Then becoming wholly engulfed in your mission you have suddenly forgotten all about the outside world. You started to believe, as that was all your senses could experience, that Mars rover was all you were.

From the day you were born here you have been told you are your body, this is your name, you are alive now and one day will die. All your senses relay information from this worldly experience. No wonder most of us had forgotten all other existences and our higher being.

Yet one day we will peel off this earthly layer, like stepping out of a dirty set of clothes. We can through tuning in and listening to its call and messages, also start to become aware of and in tune to the greater world and the Spirit of Love, which is a dimension beyond our bodies and human centred minds.

Just like the old hippie saying: Turn on, Tune in and Drop Out. We can learn to live more and more in that wonder-filled beautiful place, living from and in the being of the Spirit of Love. This is our true state, the real home of our consciousness and Divine nature.

Reach Out

> *'Reaching out to rescue one another, under any condition, is an eternal measure of Love.'*
> – Ronald A. Rasband

How about reaching out across the boundaries into another world—the world of another human being? How about finding out what they want, desire or need? That is what we do when we are in Love. Though often, out of fear we only allow that love or possibility of that love to flow through such restricted openings.

When we are in Love, we give our bodies, our minds, and hearts, our all, fully into that experience. We step into the Kingdom of Love and experience that bliss for a while. Sadly though, the cares of this world, along with our fears, our conditioning and just life often pulls us away from such abandonment. We crash back, thinking that was a dream and that we have now returned to reality. What upside down thinking! Could we have stayed there? Can we return? Most abandon those thoughts and fall back into the mundane pattern of life. They lie to themselves about the experience of bliss, often creating curtains of forgetfulness to block the pain of the missing and longing for that place of Love. Why do we often build walls with bricks of fear to protect us from such a turning upside down of the normal and experiences of aliveness?

Our task, if we are to return to that place of home, is to melt those blocks to Love and to become all we actually are, to be loving, like our true nature was designed to be.

Where or how far would a saint, maybe Mother Teresa or Princess Diana go? How far would a Goddess or Angel go? Is there a limit as to how far Love would go, or strive to keep? Would that we could remember the Love we are and we could live from that place of Love again. Our world would be a different place, freed from the bounds of fear and selfishness, neither of which is known in that perfect world of Love, the home that our deepest hearts yearning searches for, and calls us back too.

Why do we seek to restrict Love and to finding it through such a narrowly constricted window or a heart surrounded by walls, so

PART ONE: LOVE

that it becomes almost impossible to find? Love, by its very nature, is seeking expansion and oneness. Maybe we should turn our thinking, beliefs, and values inside out and upside down so we can actually discover all of our hearts deepest desires again!

A Letter to a Lover

Dearest One,

First I'd like to say I Love you deeply, and as I feel you know, from a place of deep divine love, as well as love here in the physical. I also believe and feel a part of you Loves me deeply too.

From all I have written, am learning and have experienced through many lessons. It is our thoughts and beliefs that shape and create the worlds we live in and experience. Many of these beliefs have been formed by other than our own choices, from parents, ancestors, media, and religions, also from the wrong meanings we have applied to events in our childhood. These often become the blocks and sabotages that can stop us from living a fulfilling, love-filled and inspired life—our birthright, connected with the Divine, others and our true soul calling, in our journey through this life.

I do believe it is our collective beliefs, mine and yours, that have sabotaged the beauty, the connection, passion, and fulfilment of what started as such an amazing soulmate relationship. I am so sad to see and possibly believe that it has ended and while I believe wholeheartedly in your majesty of choice. I have a problem understanding that is really the best and highest for both of our lives.

You told me that you couldn't give me the Love that I shared, I so needed, which though extremely sad, I respect, but I don't feel you have ever answered my question. If you could, would you want too? Though maybe by your choices and actions you have? I absolutely believe, if you desire it, there would open a way of healing and releasing the blocks that have caused such a turning back.

Relationships are primarily about healing, which, I'm sure is our path in our life's journey. As Marianne Williamson has shared in "A Return to Love," the secret to life and successful relationships can be found by dissolving the blocks or beliefs that hold us back from Love.

Your choice entirely, but I would like to suggest you consider

PART ONE: LOVE

looking at some of the beliefs, that I believe you may hold in some way or in similar forms and decide if they really serve your higher self and your prime life's calling – to be Love. I believe, if we choose too, we can dissolve all blocks and so rewrite our beliefs and experience a knowing of the Divine which is the Loving core of our nature. We just need to be prepared and willing to open up. I know I have at times experienced a part of you that is entirely in that place of Love, and so desire to meet you there, more and more forever.

If I haven't got any of these completely right or some have already been washed away, please look inside and see if similar beliefs resonate and are currently there for you. Then also decide if these beliefs are serving the highest parts of you or are now redundant. Where they put there in the past, for now, mistaken or redundant protection? Also, decide if you would like to replace them over time with new and more empowering beliefs. If you want to, You Can! – Whether to revive our relationship or for your future growth.

Some of these beliefs, I feel I may have encountered in your being. I am sure, I also have many beliefs to replace, I faced some more this morning!

Men just want to use me.

I need to protect my self to be safe.

Men will be just like my father.

Fears and beliefs—around having children.

The passions of Love, in early relationships, will fade.

I can't have a structure in my life without a regular job.

I don't have self-worth without a job and my own income.

It is too dangerous to commit fully.

I the ego must remain in control.

Sex is bad, and just something men want.

I can't let go, or I will lose everything.

I can't have a proper orgasm.

I don't enjoy sex any more.

I will disappear or change if I enter fully in a relationship.

I'm sure you can, if you'd like to, dig out plenty of other limiting beliefs, and I'm sure I also have many that need work and replacing. It is a continuous process and relationships are designed to help us grow through that process.

My biggest question—are you running away from Love? Is it from fear of commitment or surrender? Do you really feel your current path is Spirits path and will bring true happiness to you? Will your leaving help create and fulfil your life's purpose?

If you believe it is and will and that is what you truly desire, then I continue to wish you the very best and as before, set you totally free with my blessing.

If you feel serious doubt about that, then now is probably the time to take a different direction and decisions, a complete turnaround or metanoia and especially to ask for the Miracle of the change of thoughts. It can happen if you desire it and I would love to be with you and work together on rooting out all of our false beliefs and the thoughts that have taken us from original bliss to sadness and separation and blocked further joy and connection.

I still believe there is something wonderful that we could have created together and by amazing grace, still could. I feel there is still a chance when mixed with the sincere heartfelt desire to change all the limiting beliefs and dissolve all the blocks. It could change our worlds and potentially that of many others that we would meet and could mightily influence. Real sorry can and will create a complete change of direction!

Let me know. I believe in you.

Yours in Love

PART ONE: LOVE

Where Have All The Kisses Gone?

Dearest Lover,

Where have all the kisses gone? It seems a vast gulf has opened up between us, yet even with one that had been so close. The thoughts of a thousand cares or are they fears, turning the bliss of Love into a frozen pit, a mire of discontent. Was it the fear of future woes that stole our love, or looking back at an ever-rosier past, or maybe the necessities and details of a mundane life? Did this crazy world lead us to forget to paint each day with the bright colours of Love and send our once grateful hearts screaming out the door?

Or was it the deep wounds of our inner children crying for love, yet through past fears and blocks unable to open, let go and throw away all those perceived fears? Are we so lost in the patterns of early years that our Love was blocked and those kisses stolen?

Or maybe it was just a clash of values? Old friends yet deemed so important, written by habit and beliefs, looked upon as the foundations of who we are. Yet I know we are Love and so much more than these!

Our hearts beating, they are crying for a Love so deep, that our minds, lost in the whirring of constant thought, don't often stop to listen. Yet in a moment of silence, we can hear the call. It is a call, to come back to Love—our home, before the gates of forgetfulness and time locked us out.

Maybe together we can find the strength to cast off all burdens, the weights and hurts that hold us back? Two souls agreed, and journeying together have great power. We can, when united, cast off ten thousand demons and bathe our wounds in the wonder of forever Love.

So what can we do to find those kisses again? Let's look back and remember the joy and Love that first bloomed. Its power pulled us together out of past lonely lives. Its bliss and ecstasy built a bond, a knowing of Divine connection. A time of Love that joined our paths, but now seems just an almost forgotten memory.

Let us walk back down the path of that connection. Let's remember the very essence of the Love which once drew us together, admire its wonders, see its beliefs and feel its bliss again. Was it an illusion or was it truth that our souls were crying out in joy?

Was it a finding of the one, bringing a deep forever Love, a companion, a traveller journeying through the same wilderness—seeking a better place? Sent or given as a mirror, to seek out and discover the places that needed that touch of healing Love. Those touches, when we learn Loves lessons, are Love enough to heal our wounds, and then pour out a balm to heal the hearts of many others.

Let's live the vision and the reality of that Love, for in truth Love is all that exists. Let's open up and let its balm pour into our hearts and lives again. Let's journey through our lives once more focussing on all that is Love. The light of its beauty will make all shadows of past fears flee.

Let's blow on the embers of that fire of passion, which once was our light and in its bliss, dance together again. The fire that can melt all darkness is waiting deep inside. Blow with the breath of Love. The embers will glow and then burst into heavenly flames. Then the kisses will return and live forever.

PART ONE: LOVE

Love Shines through the Tears

'Just as hope rings through laughter it can also shine through tears.' – Maya Angelou

Surrounded by sadness, grief and seeming failure, through my tears, I refuse to accept defeat—for all these things aren't real. They are mere illusions, puffs of smoke in seconds of time, sent to bring fear, and this is not real either.

All there is, in reality, is Love and Oneness! That truth I stand on, in spite of all that appears to my dulled senses. Though they are blurred by many tears, I know the promise—that joy comes in the morning, and what a glorious morning that will be.

That is a day when there is no more sadness and the truth of Love reigns. Love conquers all fears, and the Light of its truth will shine forth, melting all darkness, in the new and promised day.

Hold on my love, hope is at hand. Love casts out all fears and will triumph!

Love—for now, the night is far spent and we have proved there can be joy and peace.

Love will return shortly and one day soon will never be cast into shadow again.

I Love You.

A Birthday Message from Love

This is a beautiful message from Love, that flowed in, in the early hours of the morning, just before a loved ones birthday.

Divine Being,

Here is a message of Love to honour your birthday or actually the day you chose to arrive on this earth, passing through the tunnel of forgetfulness into a strange and alien place.

Your actual Divine creation was in a completely different realm, a thought in the mind of God, the Divine Being, and the Energy of Love. I especially honour you for the choice to come to this world—knowing of that forgetfulness, and along with its joys, that much suffering, many lessons and learnings would be entailed.

Knowing that Salvation and Forgiveness were always your birthrights and nothing could harm your priceless being. In spite of the parched land, this journey would at times visit, all would forever be well. This is just a journey into illusion, though we are never truly separated from Love and our place in the Heart of the Divine.

Why did we come, you might ask, on this crazy ride into such an alien world? Was it so we could find and appreciate the Love we are? We are so much more than all it seems we are in this world! We are here learning, and understanding Loves depth and truths from another perspective—being seemingly apart from them. That lack and at times, seeming experience of no Love, stuck in the appearance of an illusionary time loop. Then making the majestic choice that our highest desire is to be and find the Love that we are.

Choosing to follow Love; to Love, give Love, be Love and receive Love, to desire the path of that Love and to pursue it, seems to me, the only route out of this maze of our own creation.

Keep looking towards the light in this ever darkening place. Keep the knowing that the Light of a new day is dawning and is but a few breaths away. Awakening from the dream of just a few moments in this world of time, realising it was over in the flash of knowing, remembering and enlightenment—this is our true destiny!

PART ONE: LOVE

Our temptation is to tread water hoping that day will speedily come—yet I feel there is a journey, a path of learning and Love available to follow, to hasten our escape. We can bring that awakening of Light and Love, the salvation of forgiveness fully into our world and that of our companions on this journey. Those companions are travelling in this land, as seemingly different parts of us, yet in reality, there is only the One.

I'm sending much Love to you on this special day. I honour you and Love you.

Time is short and due soon to fall back on itself, into the only true eternity of now. Our constructs of past and future, holding with them the illusions of false truths, fears and regrets are soon to be consigned back into that false illusion where they were created—as we all escape their clutches by realising how they were just fearful constructs in a crazy dream. They were ideas designed to protect us and keep us safe created by our egos—yet so opposed to the truths of Love.

Until we share again, my Love. I honour you. Enjoy your special day, celebrate your passage into this world, but also much more, your incredible journey back into the arms and being of Love. Which if the truth was known and fully remembered, you never left.

Sent with Much Love, Keith

A Message from Love

'The best proof of love is trust.' – Dr. Joyce Brothers

TRUST! You don't have to strive to create heaven on earth, your dream of a perfect place, situation or environment. You are that perfect being, your spirit lives in that perfect place and environment. It is coming. It is your birthright!

Is it Love or is it fear? It's only your fears, created from ego, that tell you that you don't have enough.—that you are not enough. You will not have enough in the future—unless you do all of these things today, to make human perfection or a safe haven for that future. There is no safe place in the temporal world of illusion; all of this is created by our ego mind, the earthly illusion, which is separation from Love. Just quit striving in that impossible place and direction! The home you desire doesn't exist in this world of fear! All striving carries you further away! You have enough for today, don't you?

Every step towards fear, or in that direction, leads to an ultimate death! One way or the other those fears must die!

All you desire exists within you—The Love you are, that Love which is God within you. Ask, in deepest prayer, with tears for the Holy Spirit to give it back to you—to help you to melt all those fears and trust. You are that place of peace when you let go of everything else and quit striving. Too long we are thinking we have to somehow create heaven ourselves in this land of illusion.

Life Loves you and wants to give you back everything you are and everything your beautiful heart desires. And no you don't have to do it or create it. You Are It!

When you get this message and learn to trust, the Sun will come out from behind the clouds of illusion and Love will shine so much brighter in your life. Gratitude will blossom, and its fruits will be picked in thanksgiving. You are Flying Back to Love.

I Love You. Your brightest future is just behind the clouds of illusion. TRUST!

PART ONE: LOVE

Self Love – Sacrifice or Selfishness

> *'Great achievement is usually born of great sacrifice, and is never the result of selfishness.' – Napoleon Hill*

I have been thinking for some time now that some of the ideas shared in this new age of enlightenment, in certain circumstances, may be leading in the wrong direction to a life of selfishness.

Now a lot is shared about loving ourselves, and yes, this is extremely important. Without the ability to love, respect, care for and admire ourselves, we are destined to a downward spiral of self-loathing, self-pity and hate. Sadly many people suffer from these mental patterns. In this context, I am all for self-love and self-respect.

However, I think the ego and its self-interest have been starting to hijack this idea. It is sometimes attempting to use it to take the unwary on a journey of egotistical selfishness. There is a time for self-care, rest and pampering, but if this becomes the first thought in our decisions, life would be taking a turn for the worst.

Some people continuously sacrifice themselves. Now, while this may also be detrimental, the great things in life have never been accomplished without sacrifice. The ultimate sacrifice, which we applaud, is the giving up our earthly life for another. Our daily sacrifices, which may be too quickly forgotten, are of exceptional merit. Life would almost cease if all our mothers had not made massive sacrifices to tend for and nurture us as we grew up. Most fathers also make the sacrifice of working hard to support their families. Voluntary and charity workers are giving time and energy, often unsung and unpaid. Where would our society be without the many Loving sacrifices and the gifts of time, money and energy?

In relationships, sacrifice and compromise are paramount to success! The modern paradigm of me first seems to be destroying the foundations of far too many marriages and relationships. Teachers on successful relationships often share that success is not just giving 50%. It's about each giving 100%, to create real and lasting success.

The Bible shares that "Love sacrifices all and is kind," and without Love we are nothing! It also promises eternal rewards for Loving. Maybe it is time to re-evaluate our beliefs and our ideas about self-love, and ask Spirit for real wisdom and balance—and especially the Love to make right choices in every situation.

PART ONE: LOVE

The Golden Rule Love!

'Though shalt Love thy neighbour as thyself.' – Jesus.

Love is all there is. It is everything! It is the Divine! When we fully realise that underneath all the illusions, which we have created in this earthly plane, on the highest levels, or maybe deepest levels, there only exists Love. If there is only Love, then that Love is us. We can do, be and have nothing else! For we are Love itself! That realisation, knowing it and owning it, in every cell of our being is the miracle. It is what some would call salvation, others may say, it is enlightenment.

As a part or children of the Divine, we can do nothing but Love. So in this dream, as a part of our return to Love, how can we Live that Love?

Realising you neighbour is yourself! All we do, feel, or even think about another, is wholly affecting and directed back towards ourselves. Some call this the cosmic law of Karma. This is where taking personal responsibility comes into the picture. When we take personal responsibility for all that we see and experience in our own universe, and we desire the miracles of forgiveness and healing; then, as the all-powerful beings we are, it will happen!

The ancient Hawaiian practice of Ho'oponopono is the perfect picture of this. In its simple form, it is encapsulated in the words: "I'm Sorry. Please Forgive me. Thank You. I Love You." In its more in-depth practice, there is a belief that we are all connected with everything. So there becomes a responsibility to maintain a Loving balance, with forgiveness and by cutting any ties that are not in that perfect unity of Love. It is a constant practice of cleansing and forgiveness. A knowing that all disharmonies are within. That they can only be cleansed using the power of Loving forgiveness, of self and of our perceptions of others. By frequently using this practice, the perfect balance of Love can be restored.

All other beings, as a part of the great mind of the Divine, in Spirit can sense our true intentions and our deepest thoughts—and us likewise theirs. It is when we become so engaged in the dream state of this world, that our intuition, a natural sense, becomes dull, or we are just not listening to it, that we spin out of control: Then, fully engaged in our own limited ego and world, we become stuck in the construct of time and fall back into its craziness. This is a black hole of our own creation, where energy can barely escape.

Fortunately, Love, forgiveness, Spirit and our Oneness are so much greater than the crazy illusionary dream. The energy of Love can melt all the black holes in our galaxies. Time is also dissolved, along with its illusions. All was never anything but whole anyway!

Thus begins and never ends the cosmic story of Love. The moral of the story; Just Love and be Love, for it is all there is!

PART TWO
SEX

'The secret ingredient to sex is Love.'
– Lars Von Trier

'I want Soul Sex.
I need to taste your thought process.
Together we can unravel riddles.
The deeper, the sweeter .'
-Unknown

PART TWO: SEX

SEX

> *'I want to undress you, touch you, kiss you, taste you. I want you hard and hot and deep and fast. And then I want you slow and sweet. I want you under me and on top of me and sitting and standing. I want to see your eyes when pleasure makes you light up. I want to hold you when you come down and try to find your breath. I want everything with you...' – Robyn Carr*

There are more fears, taboos, and shames about sex than any other part of our human life! Why is this? What makes this incredibly powerful life force such a monster, the elephant in the cupboard, which so few dare to even talk about, let alone explore its powers, meanings, and liberation? Would it be okay to explore and see the possible reasons, why the powers that be have attempted to keep us from life's pleasures, freedoms, and enlightenment?

Most of us have been so conditioned, that even the very thought of exploring anything but the most vanilla experiences send shivers of fear and condemnation screaming through our psyche. In our modern age, we often consider our selves liberated. It's true that we have come a long way, but true Loving, empowering sex, whether self-pleasuring, or with a partner, or multiple partners. Anything slightly away from, officially sanctioned, and more normal behaviour is still suffocated by many taboos and imposed shames. It is squelched by imposed fears of dirtiness, of, "what would people think," or imposed fears of isolation, by stepping away from usual, acceptable behaviours.

These things have not always been so and different cultures and civilisations have held different values and other beliefs. Some tribes live in communal quarters, sleep and make love together and share the parenthood of their children. They have very different values, with rituals of initialisation into adulthood, training in sexual awareness and even lovemaking by elders.

There have been cultures where courtesans would initiate younger men in the arts of lovemaking and keep other men's desires

LOVE, SEX, NAKEDNESS AND THE DIVINE

satisfied—those that would never have been considered by their prim and proper wives. Also, there have been times when, in some religions, women would go into the temples and use sex and lovemaking, to celebrate feast days, or for healing men, and especially soldiers returning from wars. They were showing men the Divine and sharing healing through their lovemaking. Was this purely immoral debauchery, or powerful liberation, serving a purpose in their worship and societies?

There are secrets of the power of sex, sexual healing and liberation refereed to in many writings and cultures. Those as diverse as works on tantra in ancient religions to one of the most read personal development books of more recent times, Think and Grow Rich by Napoleon Hill. Though even he feared to talk too much about the power of sex and kept it as one of the hidden secrets in his book.

Why is it that the powers that be have so demonised and sought to control the very acts, pleasures and liberating powers, which is found in its practice and participation? Could it be their fear of us discovering our divinity and then no longer needing their control and rituals? Their system only offers a delayed and promised heaven, and that only if we follow their ordained paths of good behaviour.

Why is it taught that we cannot have such pleasures, and this life is for suffering? Yet, we will qualify for heaven and its pleasures by being good and refraining here on earth. They seem to want to maintain us, in a miserable state, so we need their religions. So many of their imposed religions only offer heaven after a life of sacrifice and denial on earth. The Muslims, offer the wonders of houris in heaven, after the sacrifice of death in this life, and others, offer similar promises of future heavens when we have been duly pious and sacrificial.

While there may be many truths in the idea of living a Loving life, within the boundaries of living the Golden Rule, surely the Divine wants us to be happy and enjoy the pleasures of the now, not in some far off and illusionary future—even tomorrow never comes!

The Golden rule, according to great masters, is to Love thy neighbour as thyself, which would seem to open the doors to both self-pleasuring and pleasuring your neighbour. Though of course, there is the caveat of being aware and choosing wisely, based on how all actions would affect, or hurt third parties and others. Whatever we choose, to fit within the bounds of that Golden rule, every action and thought must flow with Love for all concerned. In this new world, when all are living the Golden rule, your neighbour would also love you, be loving and would share all things with you.

Why have our fears led us to create selfish boundaries and the walls between us when, underneath it all, we are all one anyway?

I believe there is within us, a place of the perfect being and the creation of the Divine. That is our Divinity, in pure perfection, where all the things and the fears of this illusionary world disappear. It is the place where true Love, life, and liberation exists. There we can return to the state of our original being— Divinity, where all Loving acts become natural acts, coming from the core of our Loving beings.

We can then bring those fundamental values into our lives, in this moment, which is the only moment of now. Find it within and let its power unfold into the timeless wonder of now and you.

Sex, Nudity, Freedom, and the Divine

'If we were meant to be nude, we would have been born that way.' – Oscar Wilde

Your beautiful gleaming body has millions of dedicated pleasure sensors. It has entire systems designed to release more powerful feel-good drugs than anything that can be purchased illegally. It can take you to places of divine bliss, with energy, light, and orgasm, rippling through every cell. It arrives in this universe naked in its wondrous beauty. It can provide some of the most beautiful experiences of connection with other voyagers.

Yet these systems, controls, and gauges are plagued with more false limiting programming than probably any of the other areas of command and control in our lives.

Fears, guilt, and jealousies wreak havoc on most being's voyages; and spoil, or limit many of the pleasures and experiences that, I believe, our wonderful crafts are designed to fly us through. The opportunity for heavenly bliss and connection is inbuilt, yet in so many cases, we have been sold short and end up with a quick spurt of limited sensation.

It's been said the devil hates sex but loves to promote it! The media and advertising are full of the power of sex, yet conformity programmes shout, 'don't you dare to show too much interest in it, or you are a weird, promiscuous, sex maniac, or pervert.' Why is it that the natural, physical things of connection and love are considered more obscene than hatred, war, and violence?

How did these things start? How many limiting beliefs and fears have been impounded into our consciousness? In many cases, these were shared by well-meaning parents seeking to protect us; in others, by religions and governments seeking to control us. Did it start in infancy with, 'You shouldn't touch that bit?' Or 'Cover that up, it's naughty!' Or was it the religious teachings that claim sex is only for procreation and shouldn't be enjoyed? Maybe it was the old wives' tales, which share that men are evil creatures that just want to take advantage of you. Or possibly, current fears of loss if another being was to see or enjoy the beauty of your partner. Maybe you can think of other fears or beliefs that stifle your own pleasures?

Who first taught us that some parts of our bodies were more taboo than others? Why, in some ages, was it considered too revealing to see an ankle? Yet now, sometimes, all is revealed. How come it's okay to kiss a cheek but too risky to kiss on the lips? Yet in other situations or cultures, it could be considered unfriendly not to? Why is it considered okay by most people to touch an arm, but improper to touch a breast? It's okay to pay for a massage, but whoa, a massage to touch and pleasure our most sacred bits could be considered immoral and illegal.

Yes, set your boundaries and live with them, but be careful they don't become chains that destroy the experiences and pleasures that are a part of the functions of our incredible crafts. Be sure that they are the boundaries of your choice, and not some arbitrary blockages programmed by others for a different age or situation, and held in by the fears and the penalties thus imposed.

It was the Divine that created your beautiful body and filled it with so many pleasure sensors that it's almost impossible to count them. So enjoy it, and all the pleasures and love it can bring. Life Loves You!

Tantra or Tantric Sex

Tantra

'Tantra is a pathway, not just to sexual ecstasy but to personal healing and fulfillment.' – Andrew Barnes

What is Tantra? That is a pretty deep question, and there are many answers, interpretations, and misinterpretations. Many fear it and have put in a box as some crazy sex practice. For me, Tantra is connection and breath, which is life. While tantric sex can be a part of Tantra, and I will discuss this later, it is just a small part. Just as our sexual organs are a part of the whole of our body and life, Tantric sex is only a part of the philosophy and practice of Tantra.

Tantra is about life and energy. Much of Tantra is about energy, which is the core and most important level of our beings. It is a valuable tool and one of many, which give understanding. It's a route to help unblock and get all our energies, once again, flowing in unison throughout our beings. Tantra has, within its practice, many exercises, tools, and meditations, which can connect us with our energy systems. Its practice can move us towards states of divine bliss and the understanding of our bodies, our nature, and beings. Its origins were in the East. In more recent times it has been discovered, popularised and spread by western pioneers and many explorers of life. Many of these were seeking deeper meanings and answers to the mysteries of life.

Understanding our body's energy systems, using the model of the chakras, has become a part of this and many wider systems of healing and spiritual growth. Everything on a deeper level, beyond our ordinary senses, is just energy. Rituals, healings, and meditations to unblock the energy centres are also covered by the umbrella of Tantra and other Eastern originated, practices and philosophies.

The Chakras in our physical bodies are:

The Root or Base usually represented by the colour Red.
The Sacral or Sex usually represented by the colour Orange.

PART TWO: SEX

The Solar Plexus usually represented by the colour Yellow.
The Heart usually represented by the colour Green.
The Throat usually represented by the colour Blue.
The Third Eye usually represented by the colour Indigo.
The Crown usually represented by the colours Purple or White.

See the book cover for a picture of these chakra colours in an inverted triangle, which often represents the feminine. This does not mean just the female. We all have both masculine and female energies within us.

When the energy systems are unblocked, energy can then flow freely throughout our beings, from the earth to heavenly dimensions, or from the higher realms of consciousness, back to us and the earth. It can also flow between us and others or between different parts of our beings. A Measure of control, of this energy movement, its benefits, and experiences, can then be realised. This is symbolised by and often called the Kundalini snake or Kundalini awakening. It is possible through this energy, for our consciousness to voyage on journeys through the chakras and upwards into realms of bliss. All can join together, in the form of a cosmic dance.

Breathwork also can be a big part of this liberation. Learning to control and ride our consciousness, through different breath patterns, can lead again to worlds of ecstatic, orgasmic experiences. There is magic in the space between the in and out breaths and also between the contraction, tension, and release of all the muscles in our bodies.

Understanding and using the resources of our bodies, travelling within, and into worlds beyond our primary human senses is the journey of Tantra. These and many other similar practices have been developed over ages by wise teachers, monks, and priests from many old and new traditions.

Become the explorer, check it out, you never know what magic you might discover.

Tantric Sex

> *'There is no big mystery to Tantra. It is in the allowance and grace of the breath. Breathe easy and naturally and you will open the door to a sacred intent. With this sacred intent, love making becomes spiritual and holy. You open the gateway to total joy and you embrace the divine, erotic impulse. So breathe and relax. This is tantra.'* – Janet Robertson

There is so much more bliss and ecstasy available in orgasms than that quick spurt of limited pleasure, being experienced by most men and many women. There are worlds and almost timeless explosions of rippling energetic orgasmic pleasure, which can flow through every cell in our bodies and beyond. These can be experienced, unlocked and unblocked, using tantric and other similar techniques. There can be experiences on our own, or in connection with a partner. This is where most people's limited belief about Tantra and tantric sex resides. To shatter a myth— there doesn't have to be genital sexual intercourse to attain beautiful states of connection and orgasm. At times, it can move far beyond even physical touch. Tantra is all about moving energy, in many ways and forms.

I feel that the enhanced connection, between two beings, culminating in a physical, sexual union, shared with the tantric practices of eye gazing, breath and energy work, is one of life's ultimate pleasures. This sharing and flowing together can be one of the most beautiful ways two humans can experience our true oneness and many blissful profound moments on an incredible journey of passion and knowingness along the route. It can lead to amazing wonder-filled experiences of the dancing together into oneness. This can be another way of using tantric practices to enhance our lives.

PART TWO: SEX

A Quick Spurt of Pleasure

> *'It's easy to take off your clothes and have sex. People do it all the time. But opening up your soul to someone, letting them into your spirit, thoughts, fears, future, hopes, dreams… that is being naked.'*
> — *Rob Bell*

For many people, the sex act, whether self-pleasuring or with a partner, has become a quick routine process, ending with a quick spurt of pleasure. Now there may be a time or times for a quick, passionate burst of lovemaking, but if this becomes an ever decreasing routine, it can leave so many increasingly erotic experiences, lost in such brief encounters. We then miss out on touching and connecting with our sensual, energetic beings.

While this could be almost okay for masculine beings, that can get aroused and find relief very quickly, the feminine is barely off the starting block and often left deeply unsatisfied, without her natural or emotional juices flowing. She can then be left wondering what sex is all about. Over time, this can lead to a complete turnoff, where the beautiful flower of satisfaction and pleasure is left withered and dry. A once-promising, budding flower of immense pleasures can remain as a dried up, dying, wilted bud, never flowering into the beauty of its many glories.

It would be like travelling to a tropical beach and then, just taking off your shoes and letting your feet paddle in the warm ocean. Rather than slowly immersing, allowing the warm water to engulf your being, slipping on a snorkel and swimming over the magnificent reef, exploring the colours, the beauty, the many varieties of colourful fish, swimming with turtles and other incredible creatures. Next time, diving deeper and exploring more, bursting back up to the surface breathless, rippling with the passion and inspiration from such an incredible experience. With each dive, we could be exploring new and different sensations, experiences and wonders.

So how is it for you? Are fears, habits, routines or the lack of time, destroying the depth and beauty available, in pure, orgasmic, slowly unfolding, uninhibited sex? This is true either, for self-pleasuring or lovemaking with others.

Are you taking enough time and slowly enjoying, letting the waves of arousal build up and lap into eventual crescendos of orgasmic pleasures. Are you using breath, sound, and movement? Making your touch play tantalisingly and moving through multiple zones of increasing arousal? Are you riding waves like a surfer, always seeking for that majestic unforgettable ride, before returning exhausted with quivering, rippling energy still echoing through every cell? Are you lying in a deep embrace, with self, or the incredible beautiful being that you have enjoyed that magnificent journey with? That, and much more is possible to unlock, from wonder-filled and often unknown places within.

So why do we so often settle for less? Is it old fears or habits? Was it the voice of parents or pastors saying such exploration is dangerous or immoral; such an act is only permitted for procreation, or is it just laziness and stuck routines. Any combination of these things can destroy all of the wonders that are possible; this leaves us on the shore of that unexplored ocean; thinking that just wetting of our feet is what the holiday is all about.

Now, for the masculine within or those in male bodies it may often seem enough, but especially for the divine feminine, the slow death from unfound pleasures or long forgotten past explored experiences, leaves her in a sleeping state or worse yet, with many frustrations, causing health problems or the creeping freezing of many other emotions. Our health and longevity can be hugely benefited by the wonderful and frequent positive experiences of a great sex life. Great sex helps keep many potent and health-inducing chemicals flowing through our systems. It gives peace, satisfaction and boosts so many facets of our lives.

It's sad that so many miss the benefits of great sex. It's a wonder that it isn't prescribed by doctors or supplied by health services. Is it time to defeat all taboos and fears, so we can thoroughly enjoy the depth of experience and the healings, which are available to us all?

When we mix that experience with deep Divine Love, it can then take us to many profound and ecstatic levels. Let's create it!

PART TWO: SEX

Boundaries or Blocks?

'Fear is the only obstacle that gets in the way of doing what we love. Fear holds us back from living the lives we're made to live.' - Miley Cyrus

Your boundaries are important. However, I would suggest that most boundaries around sex are actually blocks imposed by fears and old conditioning. They are frequently the voices of our parents or old religions attempting to control or keep us safe. In an ideal world, or the world of Spirit, how can there be boundaries, where all are one, there is no separation, and only the One Energy of Love exists.

So yes honour you boundaries but beware they are not the blocks of an ever-shrinking comfort zone, keeping you "safe" from beautiful experiences that could change your world.

I feel we all miss too many beautiful experiences because of old imposed fears or the norms of proper behaviours. We are also forgetting, on the highest levels that we are always safe, especially when following the voice of Love, rather than our fears.

An Ode to the Goddess

Dear Goddess,

Let me tell you a secret that I am sure deep inside you already know. You have the power of Love, the power of life and death. In the heart of your being, your womb is the temple of the birth of all life, the life-giving temple of Love. The gates of the temple are entered through the lips of joy. A wise man will find it. Not by proceeding directly to the temple, but by lingering along the route and bringing the gift, of a slow and tantalising journey there, through many meandering paths, through valleys and peaks—worshipping along his route, all the beauties of your divine nature. Gently touching and caressing the aura and erotic places of your being. Preparing along the way all the steps needed to reach, and win your divine heart, to enter into your deepest presence.

You have the gift of life and the hope of joy and connection. You have the power of life and death, the decision of the gift of ecstatic connection or the cold despair of the turning away at the temple door, those that are unworthy, who have not won your beautiful heart. Teach us how to worship you, prepare us to come into the depths of your fellowship.

As you surrender to love, you too will find the bliss of ultimate connection and joy. Your love has the power to turn a ravenous monster into a gentle giant, to bring a starving, parched soul into the land of milk and honey—feeding from your dripping lips, in a place flowing with that divine nectar.

Withhold not your love, your touch, and your blessings, for only in giving, will you also find that place of bliss. For one that withholdeth, it tendeth to poverty, but for one that giveth generously, joy is multiplied many times, into ecstatic bliss.

Yes, you can come to the temple and worship, but in truth, you are the temple. You have the power to show mankind God and many pleasures on the route to enlightenment, in your divine arms. Bring many men into your temple, in service, and let them find the peace of surrender and the gift of Love from the Divine in your being.

PART TWO: SEX

Queen of Love, I worship you. Giver of light and love, I honour you, in your beauty and seek enlightenment in the temple of your Love. I am blessed with your invitation to worship and the invite to come into your temple. I bring the gift of love, pleasure and heavenly fulfilment. A moment in your arms can be a lifetime in paradise.

In eternal gratitude.

Your servant in Love.

PART THREE
NAKEDNESS

*'Sweet, sane, still Nakedness in Nature!
—ah if poor, sick, prurient humanity in cities
might really know you once more!
Is not nakedness then indecent?
No, not inherently.*

*It is your thought, your sophistication,
your fear, your respectability that is indecent.
There come moods when these clothes of ours
are not only too irksome to wear,
but are themselves indecent.*

*Perhaps indeed, he or she to whom the free
exhilarating ecstasy of nakedness in nature
has never been eligible (and how many thousands
there are!) has not really known what purity is
nor what faith or art or health really is.'
– Walt Whitman.*

Nakedness

'Perfection is finally attained, not where there is no longer anything to add but when there is no longer anything to take away, when a body has been stripped down to its nakedness.' – Antoine de Saint-Exupery

There are several kinds of nakedness, and each is a picture of purity. We talk about the naked truth, nothing but the truth. What better way to understand this? Our naked being, with nothing hidden, nothing obscured.

Sadly, most of us have lost the ability to enjoy the freedom of being naked! Why? In most cases, it is impounded shame and all of its associated fears. Why should we be ashamed of the way we were born? Who taught us that certain parts of us were improper and should remain hidden? The man questions, "what if I become aroused?" The woman, "what if I am taken advantage of?" But what if these feelings are also perfectly natural? What if life has given us these experiences, as a part of our essential functions, some would say animal nature.

What is more natural than a man seeing the beauty of a divine female and becoming aroused? These powerful life given urges are there, to help us connect and produce more life. Initially, we were walking through the Garden of Eden, naked in our purity and in a state of just being. Love and desire, are ready to express themselves, in the act of creation—a beautiful picture of the wonders of life.

How can we return to that state of innocence? The consciousness, of beauty and Love? When we walk in Love and remember the Golden rule, we are almost there!

What if we could completely shed all the impounded shame, along with our many fears and just be in the perfect place of the wonder of now? I believe we can. Returning to the garden of Love is possible. In our core, all we are is pure Love, on a journey, learning to experience itself.

The hippie generation came close, but somehow the forces of darkness and forgetfulness, fears and greed fought back. Many dark clouds closed over that freedom. Then that brief moment of freedom, for many, was plunged again into the darkness of another night.

Each of us can awaken to the force of Love, the calling and the knowing that there is so much more. Inner truths can't be buried forever. Our true nature is forever seeking to surface from deep hidden places within. All things have been hidden for a while. Our being is now starting to find its way back from those deep and dark places. Inborn desire, to return to the Light of Love, is consciously calling us to return home. Truth can only be obscured for a while, before emerging again, in its naked purity.

Love will triumph. The grand design will be accomplished. We will return to the Garden!

PART THREE: NAKEDNESS

Waking Up Naked

*'If you want to know Love, you must allow the armor
of fear to be stripped from you, piece by piece,
until you are naked before the world.' – Teal*

One day we will all wake up naked! Is that a frightening thought? Actually, it happened once before—when we were born. So what is the big deal?

On one level, we are all naked anyway! In spirit, we are all communicating within the one mind. Those of us, who haven't dulled or have awakened, that gift of seeing, hearing or intuition, can already be in tune with the deepest emotions and thoughts of other spirit beings.

At our core, we are all one and a part of the Energy of Love, which is the essence of all there is. Some call this God, some the Universe and some the Divine. Whatever you call, or however you name that energy, is of no importance, whereas the recognition of our true beingness is all important.

Our human thought of nakedness is like a symbol. Our need to hide or our shame has been used to control us throughout the ages. This is why forgiveness and self-love are such essential steps in returning to that symbolic garden of Love, the place of purity and nakedness in every way.

If we realised everyone could see everything about us, how would we behave? And yes, in Spirit everyone can! They can sense our true spirit and intentions! Again, this is where forgiveness and the realisations that we are all alike in our frailties, human skins, our programming and human temptations are so vital. We all have, on this journey of life, stepped away from our Divinity into this earthly voyage of experience. This is sometimes the very opposite of all we actually are. Why? Could it be to appreciate our very essence and to learn the profound lessons of Love, compassion, and forgiveness, to experience miracles and shun all grievances?

The mirror of the external world reveals all of our deepest thoughts and what parts of us can be capable of. When we accept this, take personal responsibility and find grace in Love and forgiveness, we can be set free. Often this comes, through many tears or breakings, along with a letting go of many old beliefs and values. Sincere heartcry can change your world!

If we realised we are totally naked towards the other parts of ourselves, how would we behave? Maybe that would be a significant step towards truth! So many philosophers say, there is no one else in the room!

So let's live Love and dance in our naked purity, living in the one and only law of Love. As a great man said, "Though shalt Love thy neighbour as thyself." Maybe in this world of illusion and the return to truth, that other being really is us anyway!

PART THREE: NAKEDNESS

Skinny Dipping

> 'What spirit is so empty and blind, that it cannot recognize the fact that the foot is more noble than the shoe, and skin more beautiful that the garment with which it is clothed?' –
> *Michaelangelo*

It had been a sweltering hot day, and the heat was still radiating from the sun-drenched earth. It must have been after midnight, and I'd been working very hard, helping at a local fair. After finishing the energetic work of dismantling several stands, and loading the vehicles, I returned home, inspired, tired and somewhat wired. Somehow, the usual habit of finding my swimming trunks didn't control me. As I pulled off my sweaty, dirty clothes, a thrill of being naked kicked in. Jumping in, I felt the rush of water enveloping my body. As the coolness of that water engulfed me, it was cooling my heat and stimulating my energy.

There was an energetic thrill from the feeling of the naughtiness of being naked, along with arousal from the sensations coming from every part of my body. It was being touched by the cooling water, without the drag of wet clothing, holding me back. I was experiencing ripples of pleasure and a sensation of freedom. My whole being was being caressed by the water, in that different realm. I think this experience was my first energetic orgasm, when I was about sixteen.

I love being naked when the opportunity is there. Real freedom comes when there is a place of warmth, and safety and when with like-minded people who wouldn't be offended. I love swimming naked, dancing naked, sunbathing and especially sleeping naked. I think our bodies rejoice at the opportunities to be free from the weight of clothing and especially when set free from impounded, conditioned shames, that our nakedness is evil, dirty, licentious or just wrong.

When the situation is right, if you haven't, try it, get naked, explore the freedom, take a swim or a walk in the woods. You may Love it, and your body will thank you. Let go of the fear and shame, along with that self-hatred of the beautiful creation of your fantastic body. Celebrate its beauty and its every function.

Of course, always consider others who may not be ready for such freedoms. Also, be mindful of local laws. Stop worrying, too much, about what people will think, and especially about your seeming imperfections. People are usually too hung up thinking about themselves anyway.

When the time is right, that mirror work can also include standing naked and learning to Love your amazing, beautiful body. Even though sometimes wrinkled and seemingly imperfect, it carries you throughout this earthly journey. It has been with you all this time, and it deserves thanks and appreciation for all its wonders, healings and beauty. Love it and yourself, its pilot, the beautiful consciousness riding in such an incredible creation.

It is a powerful message and picture that we were born naked into this world—in purity and perfection. The sad thing is that we, along with the thoughts and fears of past generations have allowed that perfect being to create a completely messed up world. It is time to step back and dissolve these illusions. Let's get back to the naked purity of thought and the essence of our original creation.

What you think about, you will see! So be sure to think beautiful, empowering, positive thoughts. They will then radiate throughout your body and its world. Your thoughts create all you experience. It is the thoughts of yesterday that created today, so be sure the thoughts of today create a bright and a Loving future.

You can be free from shame and self-hatred when stepping into your Divine, open, original, naked purity.

PART THREE: NAKEDNESS

An Apology to Our Genitals

Dear Often Maligned Ones,

I would like to offer a public and pubic apology on behalf of man and womankind for the conventional treatment you have received. If you were a recognised minority group there would be an outcry and your publicly shamed status would have long ago been declared illegal.

Yet, as you are sacred yet shamed parts of us all, most continue to hide you as some blight and consider even the thought of exposing you an unforgivable sin, a public indecency, and to touch you so evil! Long forgotten cries of a parent's disdain still echoing deep in our hidden consciousness or was it some zealous religion threatening damnation and hell-fire for such obscenity?

Even now most hold the view that the only ones allowed to touch you should be our closest partners or married mates and then only one at a time in pure, devoted sequential order.—Kept for just the special mate.

Incredible beautiful pleasure parts you have been blessed by the divine with more pleasure sensing nerve endings that almost every other part of our being. I have learnt to worship and love you, experiencing pleasures, at the right hand of God, forevermore. Surely it is a sign when gentle touch and honouring brings such reaction within your parts. Your swelling and rising to so many pleasuring occasions or the softening and opening, leading to so many more pleasure sensors deep within.

Why should you be so maligned and feared? The chemicals that you can release into our bloodstreams and beings are more powerful than most illegal drugs. Those explosions of passionate energy fired up and harnessed can change our worlds. The kundalini snake, once released can open our spiritual pathways and start routes to set us free, setting every cell on route to explosions of pleasure and energetic star-bursts of ecstasy. Thus harnessing deep forgotten powers, long lost and blocked by the powers of shame.

Are you the very gateway to the temple of the Divine?—The

pleasure temple of ultimate knowledge and intimate connection. What if we held dear different views and beliefs and our society changed its long created views and taboos about your forbidden beauties and pleasures?

Yes, you are a sacred place, and such places should be held in great devotion but not be kept in private hidden from only the most esteemed devotees. What if we could adorn you with the finest gossamer veils, revealing your hidden beauties without fear and share your orgasmic pleasures in a land where none were left starving for connection, pleasure and both physical and spiritual Love?

I am sorry. Please forgive me. Thank you. I love you. You that have been considered the worst part of us leading to debauchery and immoral crime are in secret the best and should be the most treasured and worshipped parts of us. I pledge my troth in exposure and devotion to the liberation and freedom of past bondages and misplaced attitudes. You are a doorway to the temple of Divine love, which has been hidden by ages of prejudice and fear. I publicly apologise for your shame and isolation I will honour and love you on every occasion and create feast days in your honour once again. Let us cum in your glorious presence and truly honour all the amazing juices you produce, those that smooth our passages and create life itself.

I honour the meeting of our divine parts in the sacred temple of Love and seek to come in your Divine presence, sharing the visions and touch of your beauty.

Your servant in Love.

PART THREE: NAKEDNESS

Come to Me

> *'The Greatest Nakedness lies between
> the intimacy of two minds.' – Pavana*

In the morning, come to Me in the purity of your nakedness. Close your eyes. Shut down the noise of life and discover a hidden world beyond your senses. There is all joy and all beauty here. All things are seen, and nothing is left unseen. You are naked and yet clothed in pure Love.

There is no shame in Love. Love sees all and still loves. I see you and all of your thoughts, even though they are not real, and yes, you are still My beloved. It is impossible to hide, so why are you so fearful. Love loves the unlovely and casts its veil over countless sins.

You, in your purity, are sinless. The concept you call sin is impossible here. Sin is impossible for the actual being, which is a part of me. There is nothing but Love within. Is a dream a sin? Falling short is just staying in that lower dream world for a while. They say sin is missing the mark—the Most High, but how can you miss the Most High, when you are a part of Me? My begotten, My Love.

You think you can hide, but Love sees everything and still loves. Uncover your heart. Know that all you see, with your earthbound senses, is just a part of the dream. I can see all. I can raise you up, and open your heart, and the eye of your spirit, a lotus blossom. Come into my realm.

First, know that you are naked and still loved. In fact, I would have nothing less. Leave all your shames and your fears far behind-- back in the dream. Come and step into my realm. Don't seek to hide in the corner, under the false coverings of pride. Come back to me in the knowledge of your true beauty and magnificence; my lover, my friend, in the realm where all is seen, all is known, and we are One. Let's dance together in the light, loving together in an eternity of Love, living together in that heavenly mansion of absolute knowing. One and yet also many more. Like the mystery of a wave and yet a particle, we are One and also many. Dancing, knowing, exploring and growing!

Your earthy mind fears that you will wake up, back in the dream. Know there is no end, and I am forever here, in the moments you slip into reality, far away from forgetfulness. I am ever awaiting my Love, for you to put all illusions down. Come back soon, into the light of another morning.

The blissful moments will never end, for, in truth, they are all that is. We are naked together, forever in the arms of Love. Sleep now and thus wake up. Your illusions are just for a moment. Real life is on the other side of the veil.

I Love You.

PART FOUR

THE DIVINE

'I am in you and you in me, mutual in Divine Love.'
– William Blake

*'We came here to co-create with
God by extending love.
Life spent with any other purpose
in mind is meaningless,
contrary to our nature, and ultimately painful.'*
— Marianne Williamson

PART FOUR: THE DIVINE

Valiant Explorers

> *'We are not human beings in search of a spiritual experience. We are spiritual beings immersed in a human experience.'* - Wayne Dyer

There are many valiant Life explorers, who have broken free from the bonds of shame and fears, who are journeying into these seemingly forbidden realms.

Like other pioneers, who climb mountains, break records or explore the depths of the oceans. They are breaking convention and pushing accepted boundaries to discover powerful energies, passions and the very mechanisms of creation and Life. Most of this exploration involves inner worlds, unseen energies and the pathways of deep connection, orgasmic ecstasies and even Divine blissful experiences.

So many of us have been wounded or violated in this journey of life. Unpleasant experiences, or far worse, frequently as children, have led us to shut down in fear or trauma. Mistaken meanings and fears often create walls and no-go zones in our thinking and our maps of life. Sadly these blocks and boundaries are often designed with the intention of keeping us safe, but they can so often hinder our interactions with others. They are stifling all the wonders of this potentially beautiful Life.

If we don't forgive, especially ourselves and any others involved the memories of events, often distorted and magnified over time, can become prison cells keeping us "safe." Yet we have become bound by fears and are often missing many joys and powerful experiences--the Love and connection with ourselves, our own bodies and others. Life could be a far more fulfilling journey! Our journey is supposed to be about discovery, joy, and happiness. It now often becomes a sanitised isolation in a connection free environment.

Have all our joys, possible happiness, and ecstatic experiences been stolen by seemingly bad experiences, in an almost forgotten and a now often distorted past?

Many forms of this insidious programming, are seeking to deny our Divine beings, freedoms, experiences, connections, and Love! They are causing us to miss many of the wonders of the available human experiences on our earthly journeys. Explosions of pleasure, orgasmic rides, deep intimate connections, spiritual experiences, hidden knowledge and blissful joys are all sadly lost because a part of our being is out of control. In its desire to keep us safe, we have given it the keys to a jail cell and let it lock us in!

We have forgotten that our experiences in this life, bound by the walls of time, are just like an illusionary dream. We have been convinced that this experience is our actual reality, whereas it's all just dreamlike projections, illusions, and energies transmitted by our senses, onto the inner screen of our mind. These projections are then often falsely interpreted, by an overeager and protective ancient mind system. We have become governed and limited by pre-chosen choices and patterns.

After all of this realisation and seeming woe, there is good news. We are actually unlimited Divine Beings; consciousnesses, just experiencing this earthly world on a limited ticket. We only appear to be bound by the constructs of time and space. We have been programmed with the belief that we are mortal and will suffer and die. This is almost true on one level, but such a lie on every other! We are Divine beings, here on a journey of exploration. Our purpose is to Love, remember, appreciate and choose freedom, light, and liberation, rather than the downward spiralling pit of fear and darkness--a frigid, disempowered collapse into an earthly tomb, believing there is no hope.

Turning around is a choice! Awakening into the light is not just a possibility, but our Divine destiny. The Light is our ultimate destination. There are many who have already awakened and been transformed in an instant. There are others who are awakening, seeking the joys and happiness of our birthright, knowing that darkness and bondage is not our destination, just a brief shadow in a short night.

We are all one. As parts of us experience this liberation, it is causing a massive rise in our human consciousness. Our destiny is triumph and freedom. There are many healers, seers, shamans, and priests of this new consciousness. Help is always

PART FOUR: THE DIVINE

at hand. The teacher will come, when you are ready, and often from the most surprising places! Reading this shows you are. Just let go! Stop letting your fears steal all the priceless experiences that are waiting for you.

Let go into Love. It is ever calling. Spirit is beckoning and singing the songs of freedom. Your time is now. Nothing can hurt or destroy in Loves Holy Mountain. We are that place and being! It is your Life! Love, live and experience it fully.

No Longer a Caterpillar

> *'Never lose hope. The butterfly is proof that beauty can emerge from something completely falling apart.'*
> *– Jane Lee Logan*

Beautiful Divine, Pure Being of Love, I see you. I see the conflict between your Divine self and your strong earthly mind. This mind, driven by ego and our worldly programming is waging war, a battle for its moment of earthly supremacy. The values and programming of this world are seeking to triumph over the ways and values of Love. Know this. Its victories and values are short-lived. Its day is soon over.

The caterpillar can't remain a caterpillar for long, so you too can escape the stifling imprisoning cocoon of this world's lies and false beliefs. Its days were for but a moment. Watch and see, the triumph of Love is now here. The days of sadness, confusion, and lack are numbered. The ones of us, who are awakening are turning to help our brothers and sisters, those who are starting to become aware.

Let go of the old and embrace the new. This consciousness is not new, it is actually all we have been all along. We just chose to forget for awhile, so we could Love and appreciate all the more as we return to our place of true being.

What makes you think there is something in being a caterpillar? Yes, it had its place, as the beautiful picture of change. At its peak, it turns to mush—in a sealed tomb. The miracle of transformation then ripples through its every cell, and the change is manifest in an instant.

Hold not onto the ways of the caterpillar and its base level of being. It just roams the earth, consuming and devouring everything in its path, growing fat in its own restricted world until its miraculous day of transformation. Every cell in its being knows that the time is come to surrender, to let go and let its predestined change flow. As the creature starts the struggle to escape its restricting old cocoon, it recognises the new being it has become. Breaking through its old values and the walls containing it; it bursts into the light of a new day, expanding.

PART FOUR: THE DIVINE

Finally flying free it forgets in an instant all old restrictions. The butterfly bursts with joy into its new life, flying into the sunlight of Love and the beauty of its wonderful being.

Let go, my Love, of the old patterns, the old values, those that were imposed by this life. Let go of the values inherited from beings who shared the same programmes. They had themselves struggled in similar states. They sought to impose rules designed to keep you safe in the world as they knew it. Know they did their best, but they also lived in and shared experiences based on the only restrictive dimension they knew.

Who would you believe? The caterpillars saying, "You will die, if you seek to break through," or the butterflies calling, "Come and fly with us. We have broken through and transformed. We have found our truth and a life of freedom and Love."

Let go! Surrender! Don't struggle against this process, it is inevitable. All you would do is prolong your sleep state for a few more moments of unbearable struggle! Why? Fear not! This is life's purpose and its grand design. Yes, all you have remembered, or seemingly known is life as a caterpillar, but that does not mean that life is your destiny, or you are supposed to remain in that state forever.

Those days are far spent! A new life is at hand! The return to Love, to the inner being, which had been there all along, is inevitable. Sure you can't remember and fear flying, but its knowledge is stored in every cell of your DNA. Let go of those fears and go inside—deep within. You know that you can find all that you need.

Who you actually are, has always been alive within. It has just been sleeping for a while. Awaken now. Step into that being of light. Come forth into a new and joyful day—the day of Light, Life, and Love. Fly again with us into the sunlight. The old is passed! Celebrate, for this is now a new day.

You are a new being, and you are free. You are DIVINE!

Revealing Jewels

> *'Within each of us is a Divine Universe of Love.'*
> *- Dr. Debra Reble*

Dearest one,

I see you. I hear your sadness through the tales of past dark days. I am the explorer, the adventurer, the prospector. I find treasures in the dark places and the hidden depths of your beautiful heart.

In the darkness of distant ages, under enormous pressure jewels, crystals and precious stones were formed—the greater the pressure, the longer the dark night, the more precious the experience—that created such fine and valuable jewels. You are the crucible, the melting pot, the anvil, that has chosen to be the very place of creation. Deep within your earth, such pressure has created immense beauty. For only through these purgings can the hidden beauty, the enormous value of your true nature be forced into the light.

Strangely in such moments we often feel that terrible things are happening, but in truth, we have forgotten the master plan—the reason for it all. We are part of the divine foundry, choosing to enter dark places under that pressure, in the knowledge of the beauty that will emerge, the purification of energy, turning pure light into ever-growing crystals.

So remember, should the illusion of such darkness ever seek to return, there is in truth no reality in it, other than the refinement of character, the polishing of creation, the birth from darkness, of another facet of the wonderful gem that is concealed within your Divine heart, revealing your splendour.

As without, so it is always within. In the heart of all stars, there is an immense fire boiling under extreme pressure creating light and explosions from the energy within. In the core of the oyster, the irritation is producing the fine pearl. In your heart, that pain has created the love, the longing, the understanding, the desire to grow, learn and change. This pressure has brought forth a much purified you, emerging from the chrysalis of darkness into

PART FOUR: THE DIVINE

the glorious light of a new day. You are now exercising silver wings in the bright sunlight.

Know now, the purpose of the pressure is the refining of Love. Let this knowledge bring hope if for a while longer your feel the pressure of that darkness. Remember Love and light will soon shine through. A beautiful jewel will emerge into the light of day, to be a further adornment of your wondrous beauty.

Love is the Breath of the Divine

I received a beautiful message this morning. Love is the breath of the Divine when ..... calls, in Truth.

The pronoun, He, She, They or It just didn't seem to flow, which led to many profound questions in my inquisitive mind. Our English language just doesn't seem to be able to name or capture God at all, but then what can really describe all the wonders of such multifaceted Love.

The best I could come up with was, All of the above. After all, what sex is God? Is there sex in heaven? Ha! Now, that's a great question and another topic. I'd say Yes! However, we are asking now, is there a gender in heaven or spirit? This is also a question some people are asking themselves, seeking to define their gender, even in their physical body—sometimes with the same difficulty in answering. Maybe it's because we all have both male and female energy and spirit within us, in different levels, or dominance. Or perhaps it is just a question of focus.

In past times God was mainly spoken of as "He." In the times of a mainly male-dominated world the He was always used. I tend to feel, as Neal Donald Walsh uses, the "She," just seems better but maybe this is primarily because of my slightly more male-dominated mind and physical characteristics? The "It," doesn't seem appropriate, as this is usually reserved for things, animals or lower vibrational objects. However, God is in all of these things also. Actually, the "They," could be more appropriate as God or the Divine is comprised of all things and all people. We are all thoughts in the mind of God.

The difficulty isn't just confined to the pronoun, as we have just as many questions and names for the Divine and so many human disagreements, prejudices, and even wars about the name and identity of the All-Encompassing Being, the Most High. I googled, "the names of God" recently when writing a part of the book's introduction—and there are so, so many!

I love the straightforward, "I Am, that I Am!"

In conclusion: The Divine doesn't mind what you call ..... – So long as you call, think about and especially Love .... You are a

PART FOUR: THE DIVINE

part, and even the All as well! This is a realisation, which is also another big step of belief.

So choose which you prefer or which feels right for your beautiful heart, in this moment of now, it may be different in another now, and is indeed All of the Above, and again so much, much more.

Love is the breath of the Divine when *He* calls in Truth.

Love is the breath of the Divine when *She* calls in Truth.

Love is the breath of the Divine when *They* call in Truth.

Love is the breath of the Divine when *Love* calls in Truth.

You can fill in the blanks. Remember it doesn't matter—so long as you listen to the messages of Love and respond!

A Part of the Divine

*'We are all born with a divine fire in us. Our efforts should
be to give wings to this fire and fill the world
with its goodness.' – Abdul Kalam*

They say we are Spiritual Beings, here on an earthly journey, in an illusionary ride like a dream state. Who is the They? What created this illusory state? How can we find real peace, in a world that seems so opposite?

Deep and hidden secrets have been revealed through the words of great masters, prophets, and seers, throughout many ages. Pictures of truth, hidden in nature, dreams and inner knowing, glimpses of celestial truths, are often hidden in plain sight. Messages too are channelled by mediums and downloaded. These are sometimes more ordinary people, suddenly finding an open link with the other dimension, which is so close, yet on the other side of our collective dream.

Many great and amazing messages have come, beaming through, from beyond our flatland world. They are pictures of a multidimensional realm where everything is one, a cosmic intelligence, a universal mind, a place where all beings are part of that One, where peace and Love reign supreme.

Some spoke in parables and stories. Some in poetry with great wisdom hidden in their writings, often in a different language and designed for people living in different ages, Jesus, Buddha, Muhammad, Rumi, and Lao-tzu to name just a few. In more recent times Seth, Abraham and A Course in Miracles have been channelled. These are messages containing great wisdom, in words often more understandable for us travelling here, in recent times.

It seems like the messages are getting clearer—if we are open to hearing them. Is time running out, in its last fling, delivering such deceptive illusions? Could it be that more of us are awakening and there is not such a great need to hide the messages—lest, as in the past, others might think we are heretics and fanatics that should be burnt or stoned to death for challenging their more acceptable and deeply programmed beliefs?

PART FOUR: THE DIVINE

Science especially, with all the amazing and thought reversing discoveries of Quantum Physics and inner biology, has now come so much closer to the messages of the mystics. Both now seem to be sharing the same answer. We all are just energy! In fact, all that exists is composed of energy. That energy is all One. It is an amazing soup, of buzzing, moving vibrant thought—One Divine mind!

The Course in Miracles teaches we are a thought in the mind of God, a part of the whole, now for a time drifting in an illusionary world of ego. This world was created by misplaced thoughts, in that dream state. Yet, we are ever able to wake up, back into our original reality, guided by a special inter-dimensional force it calls the Holy Spirit which was left in our world by the Divine, as a bridge back to the truth. That Spirit is ready for us when we get fed up, playing the ego game that seeks to destroy us and the illusionary world we live in.

This, along with many other similar messages, makes total sense to me. In the place of my heart and inner knowing these messages resonate and ring clear sounding bells from Divine truths. It is like a knowing unfolding inside, clearing the haze of that old dream and bringing answers, a new reality, and peace. The route, to a long-missed home, is emerging from old fogs. At times I am standing in Love, on the top of the mountain, in the light of a glorious dawn, watching the mists of a cold night evaporating, exposing all the beauties of valleys, rivers and forgotten wonders of known landscapes, which were previously lost in time.

So who are the "They," that have shared such wisdom? And how can we hear them more clearly? They are a part, of that amazing collective consciousness, the many who have walked this journey before, and now stripped of illusion, naked in truth, inhabiting that place of pure energetic Love, "They," are looking through ever opening channels, to influence and share direction with all who are seeking and awakening.

That collective consciousness is, in reality, all that exists. It is our great and communal mind, the Divine, God, the Universe or whatever you would like to name it. It is all One, and there is, in reality, nothing else, in the infinite room. Yes! The greater You is that energy! In spite of this earthly illusion of billions of independent parts, the shocking truth is, that on that a much higher level, there is only One of us here!

Have You Discovered that Amazing Oneness?

Tune in, deep inside your being and explore the inner worlds of truth and peace that are hidden there. Everything in the outer, upside down, diminishing world, will eventually morph into that place of Love! Are You ready for that amazing ride?

From a worldly perspective, it is feared and called death. We can, however, experience glimpses of that state without dying. That death is also just a part of the previous illusion, as the eternal life force we are can never die. Let's live in the magical, miraculous state of the knowledge of that world. We can create many miracles of changes, in thought, by loving all that is around us, thus dispelling the myth and dream of all past disconnectedness.

Our new life of Love is here and now!

Our task is, to Give Love, Be Love and Receive Love!

And yes, a great way to start is sharing that with yourself, by forgiveness and self-love. Then help it to spread out to all the seeming others and overflow into all that is in our world, our universe and beyond.

Live Love!

PART FOUR: THE DIVINE

Words from the Divine

> *'As you awaken to your divine nature, you'll begin to appreciate beauty in everything you see, touch and experience.' – Wayne Dyer*

Step out of the darkness my children, for the day is coming and the night is far spent. Lift up your eyes and see the dawn of a new day.

The light of the sun will flood your being and cleanse from every vestige of those dark days. Not only is it a new day, and the end of a dark night, but it is the beginning of a new age—the age of Light and Love. It is time to fly!

Come and fly with Me. Spread your wings and ride on unicorns into the light. Former things are passed away. Behold the new day is here. The reign of Love is at hand. You are my ambassadors, my Lightworkers, my Love workers.

Be lights in the darkness, and the last of that darkness will flee. Open your arms, your hearts, your eyes, and you will receive and see the blessing that is to pour out in my Light. The new day has come!

The Divine

'It is within you that the Divine lives.' – Joseph Campbell

I believe we came from Love, we are Love and that we are in the process of returning to Love! Yet, at the start of this earthly journey, we chose to enter a state of forgetfulness, especially forgetting our true self, as a part of the Divine.

People have used many names for the Divine—Love, God, Allah, The One, The Universe, the Great Spirit to name a few. Sadly most of these names have been corrupted in our minds and thoughts in association with religions, fears, and prejudices. Hatred and false sometimes corrupted beliefs are seeking to keep us from finding, or remembering the enlightenment of realising our true selves and our place as a part of that ultimate everything.

As there is only one whole, therefore, all things must be a part of that one whole, and thus all things are one. For me, the best word picture that can describe the almost indescribable is the Universal Energy of Love. According to great teachers that energy or God has stated, "I Am, that I Am." "I Am" is the very name of God. We all get lost in the frailty of our human minds and understanding in attempting to picture or describe the Everything, which is so immense and all-powerful, that it encompasses All.

The beauty is we don't need to! As we seek inside, there is the knowing and link to an all-powerful Spirit, that can give us momentary glimpses and knowledge of the peace, Love and blissful happiness of our connection and place in that Divinity—and at times so much more than even that!

Sadly, in our western societies, we have often had our picture of God corrupted by the image of an angry deity. This deity is pictured as a type of super male figure, living in the clouds, seeking judgement and delivering hell, suffering and damnation, as punishment for our many sins. That is unless we buy our way out with forgiveness, repentance, suffering, devout poverty and obedience, along with numerous acts of penance. No wonder many peoples image of God is so messed up. they just don't believe or even want to know. If that were my God, I wouldn't

PART FOUR: THE DIVINE

want to know either! Some other religions share that the ultimate is a kind of nothingness void or an absence of being. That doesn't sound much fun either. How can everything ever be nothing?

So unless anyone comes up with a better picture, I will settle with Loving Energy and The Divine. Choose your own and find the wonderful Being within, through the special link of Spirit, bridging dimensions and our carnal minds, moving us into the timeless being of All Things. Its majestic experiences are available to all. They surpass all languages cultures and states. Even in our seeming individuality, there is a place and enlightenment for us in the Great Oneness of Being.

Heaven, Bliss and all the things our Divine Spirits seek to find or remember are there for us all. Young children have barely left and often still remember. Look into the eyes of babies. These things are often far too complicated for our sophisticated adult minds. Yet deep within, so many amazing truths are found in the stillness of meditation, the beauty of nature, the pictures and signpost left by wise teachers and the illustrations painted in the skies. Loves truths are just a breath away. All that seek will find. If you haven't discovered them yet, just ask, if you have, go back frequently and bathe in that place of knowing. Time is short, and our return homecoming is soon.

Celebrate with a heart full of gratitude and LOVE!

How Can I Serve?

A message for me, and all, who may find it and listen.

So you have found the Divine, that All encompassing beautiful Spirit of Love in the deep places within. What next?

Each of us has unique talents, a mission, a calling and a life purpose. We came here to remember who we are and to make the right choices, based on our desire for Love and Light, to overcome the confusion and darkness of this world. We are waking up from a deep sleep when previously lost in our own world of illusion. Now is the time to stand up for all we have found and all we have come to believe. It's time to be the vessel, which forgiveness and Love can shine through, to touch and lighten our world.

It is time to look within and daily ask, "How can I serve?" Like the beautiful prayer of St. Francis. "Make me an instrument of thy peace." There is a whole world waiting to be healed and transformed by the Love, which is now coming alive within you.

Much of this will still be through the inner daily work of prayer, and forgiveness. Melting all the past and present grievances, which are living in our memories and hearts. This is done by sending Love, blessings, and healings. I'm sorry. Please forgive me. Thank you. I love you. Use this powerful prayer to take personal responsibility for all you see, feel and experience in your world.

Much is about asking, "How can I serve the Love I am becoming?" "How can I help Love flow out into my world?" Sometimes it's a look, a smile, a word of Love, or a hug, that is shared with the right person, at the right time. Sometimes it's a prayer or a stream of healing energy sent to another. Sometimes it's an act of Loving giving. Ask Love and Love will guide. Sometimes it becomes about taking a stand and speaking your truth.

Make sure whatever you do; it is done, in Love. Seek in humility, to be sure the old ways and the ego doesn't attempt to come back in, bringing with it, its selfishness and control. Forgiving yourself, for the years spent in darkness, is an important step too.

Most of all trust and ask continually for Love to guide. How can I

PART FOUR: THE DIVINE

serve, inspire, give or forgive, manifest and be that Love? Love will show you how best to serve. That service is your calling, each day and in every moment.

For when you truly Love, You are becoming the Divine.

SOME QUESTIONS AND REFLECTIONS

What if you knew and fully believed you were a part of Love? Would it change your life?

How often do fears and shames block your happiness?

Have you managed to practice any of the Self Love exercises? Would you like too?

Have you completely forgiven your self and others, for all perceived grievances?

Take a personal inventory. How free are you? Has reading these messages helped melt some of your blocks?

How much have the fears and shames of sex hampered your joys and freedoms in life?

Have you been able to get naked and Love the being you see in the mirror?

Given the opportunity would you like to get naked and dance an ecstatic dance with Love?

Has reading this book helped and given a desire to explore more of these areas?

If so what do you plan to do about it?

What if you genuinely felt your heart and source was a part of the Divine. What changes would this create?

Many peoples biggest fear is the fear of death. What if you could believe the experience could be just like shedding old worn out clothes?

Are you looking forward to the day when all will be one, and we all feel at home again?

If any of these questions brought tears to your eyes, celebrate and know your desires and hearts calling are the first steps towards change, forgiveness, and our destiny, which is Love.

IN CONCLUSION

Just Love!—Give Love, Be Love, Receive Love.

We are moving rapidly towards the realisation that the world we live in is the big illusion! The world beyond our human senses is the only real world, and we can dwell in, and from that place of Love more and more!

I believe, I am a thought of Love in the Mind of Love and that we are all thoughts of Love in the Mind of Love—all a part of the Oneness of Love. Resting in that perfection we will see our worlds change!

As more of us wake up to these realities, the shift is occurring, and our changes are creating a global change in all around us. Most of this is through the inner work of Love, forgiveness and mind change, moving to the place of heart centred living.

The word Love appears over 500 times in this book. I urge you to wrap yourself in every facet of Love, live it and give it, it will help speed our return to our ultimate state which is Love.

Let's do our part and Stand Up for Love. It will change our world and the universes of all around us. It will help us to dwell once again in the heavenly places of our true nature.

I look forward to meeting you there as individuals and yet parts of the One.

CONNECTIONS

Soon to be available—I'm recording an audio copy of the book. Watch out for news of this. It will be available through the books website and on Amazon, Audible and other audio book platforms.

Resources and Links. – Use them to stay in touch.

My Facebook pages:
www.facebook.com/LSND.info
www.facebook.com/TakeControlofYourSpacecraft
www.facebook.com/TheLittleBookofLove.info
www.facebook.com/KeithHiggs1

Please add likes to these pages if you haven't already. If you Loved the book a review on Amazon, or other book sites would help others to find it and benefit also.

My author, books and blog sites:
www.KeithHiggs.com
www.FlyBacktoLove.com
www.LSND.info

Please stay in touch by joining to the mailing list on one of these sites.

I'm also the administrator of a public Facebook group 'Awake Your Dreams.' You may like to join us there. It is full of inspiring pictures and quotes, posted by many members. It would be great to see your favourite quotes and meet you there.
www.facebook.com/groups/AwakeYourDreams

Follow on Twitter: @FlyBacktoLove

Instagram: www.instagram.com/Keith_Higgs_FlyBacktoLove

I am available for talks, workshops and private sessions.

Contact me at: Keith@FlyBacktoLove.com

RECOMMENDED READING

A Return to Love – Marianne Williamson.

Enchanted Love – Marianne Williamson

A Course in Miracles

Finding Your Soul Mate with Theta Healing – Vianna Stibal

Take Control of Your Spacecraft and Fly Back to Love – Keith Higgs

The Little Book of Love – Keith Higgs

Life Loves You – Robert Holden

Love for No Reason – Marci Shimoff

Sacred Sexuality – Michael Mirdad

Conscious Loving Ever After – Gay & Kathlyn Hendircks

Sacred Sexual Healing. The Shaman Method of Sex Magic – Baba Dez Nichols & Kamala Devi

The Afterlife of Billy Fingers – Annie Kagan

There are also many recommended books, which helped my growth through the wonderful journey, before writing this book. A list of these is in the recommended book list in my first book "Take Control of Your Spacecraft and Fly Back to Love."

This list is available to view at:

   http://www.FlyBacktoLove.com/recommended-books

ABOUT THE AUTHOR

Keith Higgs has lived an interesting and exceptional life.

A hippie search for truth; twenty years of International Christian-based voluntary work; Editing and publishing talks and inspirational audios; Building a successful computer business—then watching it crash; Two marriages, eight children and six stepchildren; Building a MLM business, Learning from the masters of personal growth; Attending and assisting at talks and workshops; Studying NLP, healing and speaking skills; Building a social media platforms of thousands; Travelling many countries.

His combined skills, common sense, learnings and accumulated wisdom have flowed into his first two books *Take Control of Your Spacecraft and Fly Back to Love - a Manual and Guidebook for Life's Journey,* and *The Little Book of Love.*

Further studies of 'A Course in Miracles,' Tantra, Conscious Sexuality and other fields—Learning, reading and attending many workshops and festivals, also opening further to meaningful words flowing in, often in the early hours of the morning, has led to this collection of empowering messages. *'Love, Sex, Nakedness and the Divine - Messages from Love to Empower and Enlighten Your Journey.'*

Here is a man who has lived and learnt. He has a passion to share his truths, values, and beliefs with many.

OTHER BOOKS BY KEITH HIGGS

To Get Your Paperback copy, or the eBook.

Visit: www.TheLittleBookofLove.info

Copies can be purchased there, through Amazon,
or ordered through any good bookshop.

To Get Your Copy, Read or Listen to the Full Book or to get the eBook.

Visit www.FlyBacktoLove.com

A free Explorer Membership of the interactive website is available. Full Lifetime Membership is only £10. It includes a download of the Audio Book, eBook and the opportunity to read an illustrated version of the "Take Control of Your Spacecraft and Fly Back to Love" online.

Copies can be purchased there or through Amazon, Audible or any good bookshop.

ONLINE COURSE

The course is for anyone wanting to understand and melt their blocks to Love. It includes video taken from a talk I shared at the Soul Cafe and white board animations, along with lots of great questions and tools to help on your journey.

Course Criteria:

Be open to change. Have a desire to connect with yourself at a deeper level. You may feel that you need to be more loving. You may have a desire to understand why, in spite of your best intentions, your life is not unfolding as you'd like.

SPECIAL OFFER

A Discount Code for readers of this book is **FBTLDISCOUNT**

Or follow this link:

www.udemy.com/FlyBacktoLove/?couponCode=FBTLDISCOUNT

Notes

Notes